"By focusing on the impact of the fundamental principle of 'reciprocity' in the practice of international water law, this ground-breaking book explores the realpolitik of water diplomacy, highlighting the self-interest of States in engaging in transboundary water cooperation. It provides a novel, yet highly valuable framework within which to analyse and understand the approach of China, as probably the single most important State actor in the practice of transboundary water law today."

Owen McIntyre, *School of Law, University College Cork, National University of Ireland, Ireland*

"Reciprocity, China, transboundary waters – three hot topics, examined here in an innovative legal study, offering fresh insights into the complex issues integral to transboundary water cooperation. Reciprocity – over-looked, under-studied – is integral to understanding not only China's transboundary water practice, but also right across the field."

Patricia Wouters, *Director, International Water Law Academy, Wuhan University, China*

Reciprocity and China's Transboundary Waters

Utilizing the principle of reciprocity, *Reciprocity and China's Transboundary Waters: The Law of International Watercourses* analyses the past, present and future of the law of international watercourses with a particular focus on China.

As a legal principle, reciprocity plays a strong role in the formation, interpretation and maintenance of international law. Implementing this framework, the book examines the development of the law of international watercourses, highlighting how this basic legal principle is a foundational notion. It applies the framework to China and offers insights into one of the most important transboundary states in Asia. As a primarily upstream state, China is of great significance to its transboundary neighbours; however, there remain significant hurdles, misunderstandings and mistrust between China and its neighbours. China is faced with a complex challenge – how to meet its own development needs while also taking into consideration its primarily downstream neighbours? By focussing on this prominent state this work not only fosters a greater understanding of the law of international watercourses within China, but also clarifies and challenges current perceptions of China's transboundary water treaty practice. More generally, the book provides a past, present and future view on international watercourse law, starting with an analysis of the UN Watercourses Convention and UNECE Water Convention leading to a discussion of reciprocity's continued influence as well as charting a path forward.

This book will be of great interest to legal students and scholars with an interest in international watercourses, environmental politics and international law, as well as students and scholars interested in Chinese politics and natural resource management and conflict.

David J. Devlaeminck is Lecturer at the School of Law, Chongqing University, China.

Earthscan Studies in Water Resource Management

Water, Technology and the Nation-State
Edited by Filippo Menga and Erik Swyngedouw

Revitalizing Urban Waterway Communities
Streams of Environmental Justice
Richard Smardon, Sharon Moran and April Baptiste

Water, Creativity and Meaning
Multidisciplinary Understandings of Human-Water Relationships
Edited by Liz Roberts and Katherine Phillips

Water, Climate Change and the Boomerang Effect
Unintentional Consequences for Resource Insecurity
Edited by Larry Swatuk and Lars Wirkus

Legal Rights for Rivers
Competition, Collaboration and Water Governance
Erin O'Donnell

Water Allocation Law in New Zealand
Lessons from Australia
Jagdeepkaur Singh-Ladhar

Reciprocity and China's Transboundary Waters
The Law of International Watercourses
David J. Devlaeminck

Water Management in China's Coal Power Sector
Xiawei Liao and Jim W. Hall

For more information about this series, please visit: www.routledge.com/books/series/ECWRM/

Reciprocity and China's Transboundary Waters

The Law of International Watercourses

David J. Devlaeminck

Routledge
Taylor & Francis Group
LONDON AND NEW YORK

earthscan
from Routledge

First published 2021
by Routledge
2 Park Square, Milton Park, Abingdon, Oxon OX14 4RN

and by Routledge
52 Vanderbilt Avenue, New York, NY 10017

Routledge is an imprint of the Taylor & Francis Group, an informa business

British Library Cataloguing-in-Publication Data
A catalogue record for this book is available from the British Library

Library of Congress Cataloging-in-Publication Data
Names: Devlaeminck, David J., author.
Title: Reciprocity and China's transboundary waters : the law of international watercourses / David J. Devlaeminck.
Description: Milton Park, Abingdon, Oxon ; New York, NY : Routledge, 2021. | Includes bibliographical references and index.
Identifiers: LCCN 2020025945 (print) | LCCN 2020025946 (ebook) | ISBN 9780367249793 (hardback) | ISBN 9780429291753 (ebook)
Subjects: LCSH: Water resources development–Law and legislation–China–History. | Water-supply–Law and legislation–China–History. | Water rights–China–History. | Water rights (International law)–History.
Classification: LCC KNN3046 .D48 2021 (print) | LCC KNN3046 (ebook) | DDC 341.4/480951–dc23
LC record available at https://lccn.loc.gov/2020025945
LC ebook record available at https://lccn.loc.gov/2020025946

ISBN: 978-0-367-24979-3 (hbk)
ISBN: 978-0-429-29175-3 (ebk)

Typeset in Bembo
by Wearset Ltd, Boldon, Tyne and Wear

To Yun

Contents

Acknowledgements

This book is the product of a long journey that began in Hamilton, Ontario, Canada where my interest in transboundary water issues first sprouted while completing graduate studies at McMaster University and the United Nations University – Institute for Water, Environment and Health. It was my then co-supervisor, Zafar Adeel, who pointed out the opportunity to complete PhD studies in international water law in Xiamen, China. After travelling to Xiamen University to attend a conference, I decided to move there to pursue my PhD under the supervision of Professor Patricia Wouters and Professor Huiping Chen. It is there where this work began as my PhD thesis. Sincere thanks are owed to both of them for their patience, guidance and stalwart support.

Many have contributed to this work both directly and indirectly along the way, and I owe a debt of gratitude to scholars around the world who commented on this work, especially Owen McIntyre, Sergei Vinogradov, and Otto Spijkers. Thanks are also owed to those who completed their PhDs alongside me, including Nabaat Tasnima Mahbub, Farnaz Shirani, Flavia Rocha Loures, Konstantin Volkov and Judith Schöne. Special thanks to Su Yu and Kenneth Kang who were always available to read and discuss my work, and also to help escape it from time to time. Sincere gratitude also to the China Scholarship Council, without their support my PhD studies and this book would not have been possible.

This work was completed after taking up my position at the School of Law, Chongqing University in Chongqing, China, and I would like to express my deep appreciation to all the faculty and staff at the School of Law for providing the necessary environment to complete such work. Special thanks also to the Fundamental Research Funds for the Central Universities (Project No. 2019 CDJSK 08 XK 07) for their generous support in this endeavour.

Thanks to the entire team at Routledge, especially Hannah Ferguson and John Baddeley for their tireless effort throughout the process. A debt of gratitude is also owed to the various journals where aspects of this work had been previously published for their support in strengthening this research, and for their permission to utilize that work here.

Above all, heartfelt thanks are owed to my wife, Yun, who has been by my side since the very beginning. Finally, thanks also to my parents, siblings, friends and relatives in Canada for supporting me and my move to China, tolerating my absence and offering a heart-warming welcome upon my visits home, although they do not happen often enough.

Abbreviations

ARSIWA	Draft Articles on Responsibility of States for Internationally Wrongful Acts
EIA	Environmental Impact Assessment
ICJ	International Court of Justice
IJC	International Joint Commission (Canada–USA)
ILA	International Law Association
ILC	International Law Commission
LMC	Lancang-Mekong Cooperation Mechanism
MoU	Memorandum of Understanding
MRC	Mekong River Commission
PCIJ	Permanent Court of International Justice
POW	Prisoner of War
RBO	River basin organization
SDG	Sustainable Development Goals
UN	United Nations
UNECE	United Nations Economic Commission for Europe
UNGA	United Nations General Assembly
USA	United States of America
VCDR	Vienna Convention on Diplomatic Relations (1961)
VCLT	Vienna Convention on the Law of Treaties (1969)
Water Convention	Convention on the Protection and Use of Transboundary Watercourses and International Lakes (1992)
Watercourses Convention	Convention on the Law of the Non-navigational Uses of International Watercourses (1997)
WTO	World Trade Organization

1 Introduction

International relations have never been more complex, and revisiting the underpinnings of these inter-state interactions has never been more important. Largely absent from this discourse is the legal notion of reciprocity. Given that international law is grounded in the duty to cooperate as firmly reflected in Article 1 of the United Nations (UN) Charter, understanding how reciprocity informs the norms of law in this field can offer new insight into one of the most significant and pressing challenges of the present day – the cooperative management of the world's shared freshwater resources. As one of the most populous nations, soon to be the world's largest economy, China has been selected as the case study for this work. In examining the legal notion of reciprocity within the context of China's transboundary water cooperation, this work will explore the international law that governs shared freshwaters using this unique analytical approach. Not only reciprocity the foundation of international cooperation and law, but it is particularly relevant in the context of China's transboundary waters, where it has been utilized to expressly highlight the need for a "universal understanding of reciprocal rights and responsibilities," recognizing that upstream China, like all riparians, "has reciprocal rights and responsibilities" (Tian & Liu 2016).

States appear to have accepted reciprocity, with a "gradual evolution towards positive reciprocity and cooperation" since the Peace of Westphalia (Fard 2016: 11). Within international law, reciprocity has been recognized as a legal principle (Crawford 2012; Orakhelashvili 2019; Simma 2008). As such, it is the "principle leitmotiv, a constructive, mitigating, and stabilizing force, the importance of which can hardly be overestimated" (Simma 2008: para. 1). What is reciprocity? Described as "the vital principle of society" (Molm 2010: 120), reciprocity embraces three key elements: an *exchange* that is *contingent* and, at least roughly, *equivalent*. In social relations, reciprocity is prevalent at one level or another in nearly all of our interactions as a "basic, polymorphic and pervasive pattern of human social conduct" (Kolm 2008: 11). As a principle of societal exchange and cooperation, reciprocity assists in the formation of social cohesion, driving people to help those who have helped them, and not to injure those who have helped them. Ensuring this reciprocation is the gratification of receiving but also, over a period of time, the internalization of the norm of reciprocity, a process that establishes a sense of obligation between the giver and receiver (Gouldner 1960). This process of exchange establishes both balance and imbalance between participants, requiring a continuing reciprocal exchange to correct the imbalance (Kolm 2008). Although such exchange often involves a sense of equivalence, exact equivalence is often not required (Gouldner 1960).

The notion is not limited to the social context, but has been found to be a prominent factor of inter-state relations. States, as collections of individuals sharing common values, make up the international community (Fard 2016). Within the community-of-states model, reciprocal exchange has been shown to play a strong role in the establishment and support of global cooperation (Frank et al. 2018). In state-state relations, reciprocity takes on a similar meaning as reciprocity within person–person relations; however, it has often been discussed in terms of specific and diffuse reciprocity. Specific reciprocity involves an exchange of equal value where the rights and obligations of parties are very clearly laid out. Diffuse reciprocity, however, involves a definition of equivalence which is less exact, with a sequence of events that is not so readily defined. As such, it can be viewed as "an ongoing series of sequential actions which may continue indefinitely, never balancing but continuing to entail mutual concessions within the context of shared commitments and values" (Keohane 1986: 4). Such diffuse reciprocity requires states to "contribute one's share, or behave well towards others, not because of ensuring rewards from specific actors, but in the interests of continuing overall results for the group of which one is a part, as a whole" (Keohane 1986: 22). These two forms of reciprocity are not unrelated, as consecutive actions of specific reciprocity over a period of time can ultimately build trust between states and lead to cooperation based on diffuse reciprocity. As such, in inter-state relations reciprocity can also be viewed as "*exchanges* of roughly equivalent values in which the actions of each party are *contingent* on the prior actions of the others in such a way that good is returned for good and bad for bad" (Keohane 1986: 8).

While reciprocity is often associated with cooperation, it contains both positive and negative aspects. For example, in the Prisoner's Dilemma, a model used in game theory, players will always benefit individually from non-cooperation regardless of the actions of the other player, whereas cooperation will benefit both (Axelrod 1984). If the game is played as a one-time interaction between agents it will always be beneficial to defect; however, relationships between both individuals and between states are almost never a one-time interaction (Badcock 1998). In situations where states or individuals reciprocate positively with each other, returning cooperation for cooperation, mutually beneficial relationships can flourish. When an agent defects, however, then the relationship can become strenuous, potentially leading to conflict. It can also bring a sense of order to social and political systems, as this dual nature of reciprocity, its positive and negative aspects of good-for-good and bad-for-bad, provide an incentive for cooperation and a disincentive for defection (Niv-Solomon 2017). This is reflected in social relations, for example, as norms are enforced reciprocally via social disapproval and ostracism (Elster 2011). Thus, reciprocating bad-for-bad in a one-off event can act as a deterrent to greater defection (Kolm 2008). If the game is repeated over and over again a strategy of reciprocity can, over time, establish long-lasting cooperation which can defend itself against defection (Axelrod 1984). It should not be assumed, however, that relationships always begin with positive cooperation, and such negative reciprocity runs the risk of establishing a cycle of negative interaction and potentially ongoing conflict between states (Niv-Solomon 2017).

Law offers a positive framework for cooperative relationships accompanied by a negative framework of sanctions in response to violations (Schneeberger 1949), helping to ensure that, unlike the Prisoner's Dilemma, the payoff for defection is lower than cooperation, even if it were a one-time interaction (Badcock 1998). Legal systems are more than just a system of rules, but can be conceptualized as a system of legal relationships, a social phenomenon concerned with the relations between groups that are expressive of and rooted in the communities from which they emerge (Cotterell 2006; Krystufek 1974). Law itself can be described as a reciprocal, triangular system with the law at its peak, community members at both points of its base, and the equal sides representing the equality between subjects. These subjects of law each agree to participate in the legal system so long as others agree to do so, making them "co-participants in a cooperative system for mutual advantage" (Kedar 2012: 209–10). This reciprocal nature of law contributes to the rule of law, based upon the law's legality, consistency, legitimacy and sense of justice (Fard 2016). Reciprocity plays a particularly strong role in the notion of justice acting as a justificatory factor of law, such that "law can only be justified if it fulfils the requirements of reciprocity," particularly that of a fair exchange (Westerman 2014: 172).

As both a product of, and framework for, interactions between individuals as well as states, reciprocity is not only present in domestic law where it acts as a foundational notion of contract law (Hutchison 2013) and tort law (Taekema 2014), but also in private international law, most notably in the reciprocal recognition of court judgements (Lenhoff 1956), and public international law where reciprocity is a legal principle (Crawford 2012; Simma 2008). Legal principles are considered to be "unwritten legal norms of a wide-ranging character" that are found in domestic law and can be translated onto the international stage (Zimmerman et al. 2012: art. 38, para. 254). Acting as "a general normative proposition considered to be expressive of the *ratio* of a series of more detailed rules" (Zimmerman et al. 2012: 872), legal principles, as identified in the *Case of the S.S. Lotus*, are "in force between all independent nations and [...] therefore apply equally to all the contracting Parties" (PCIJ 1927: 17). "General principles of law as recognized by civilized states" are recognized as a source of international law in Article 38(1c) of the Statute of the International Court of Justice (ICJ). Although the utilization of general principles as a "source" is the topic of some debate

(Mazzeschi & Viviani 2018) they are recognized as having a variety of functions, including: 1) as a tool of interpretation; 2) as a method for the development of new norms; 3) as a supplementary source of international law; and 4) as a modifier of international legal rules (Bassiouni 1990). In line with this, the principle of reciprocity has been recognized to play a role in the creation of international law where it limits state claims; it is considered to be "at work behind all international treaties concluded freely on the basis of sovereign equality" (Simma 2008: para. 5) as a mechanism that informs and shapes the distribution of rights and duties, advantages and disadvantages of state parties, ensuring that the rights of one are the duty of the other, and vice versa; and it also contributes to the enforcement of international law via legal mechanisms, such as retorsion, reprisals and non-performance and within various dispute settlement mechanisms (Simma 1989, 2008). Although often associated with an older international legal paradigm of bilateralism and a state-centric legal system, so long as the international legal system is horizontal, based on sovereign equality and without a central authority, reciprocity will continue to be of vital importance. Over the past few decades, however, international law has, in many ways, been shifting from a law of coexistence to a law of cooperation, taking into consideration a variety of community interests via the rise of human rights and international environmental law, among others. Such changes bring the importance of reciprocity into question, as these norms do not necessarily function in a reciprocal way. With growing global uncertainties and increasing nationalism in response to rapidly evolving national and regional issues, it seems likely that reciprocity will maintain its role as the *principle leitmotiv* even as the international community works to solve today's most pressing global issues.

China and its transboundary waters

After opening up, China's economy has expanded rapidly, lifting millions out of poverty, creating a new middle class and increasing the quality of life for many of its citizens. In 2011, China surpassed Japan to become the second-largest economy, and, in 2014, China became the world's largest trading nation (China Daily 2011; Monaghan 2014). Even though economic challenges loom large, given its current trajectory China appears destined to become the world's largest economy. China's rising status in the world and the current geopolitical climate has led other states to insist on reciprocity with China as they reassess their global relationships (Chow & Sheldon 2019; Escritt & Blenkinsop 2019). It has also put significant strain on its water resources, as China is experiencing issues of both quantity and quality. Such rapid economic development has been accompanied by an increase in water usage, and between 1949 and 2008 China's water use grew from 103 billion m^3 to 590 billion m^3 (Chen 2016). China is ranked 6th in the world in terms of its total water resources, but due to its large population it is ranked 121st for per capita supplies of water, with only 2100 m^3 per capita, less than a quarter of the world average (Chen 2016; GWP 2015). China's water resources are unevenly distributed throughout the country, with greater water resources in the South in comparison to the dry North (Moore 2013). As much as 60% of China's groundwater is considered to be polluted, while some studies have indicated that 40% of China's river water is "seriously polluted" (Kaiman 2013, 2014). All of this is exacerbated by climate change, which will increase desertification in China's North and West, and potentially impair infrastructure across the country (VornDick 2015). China has thus far aimed to resolve these issues through massive infrastructure projects such as the South-to-North Water Transfer Project, the use of groundwater resources (ESG 2016), a series of environmental initiatives in China's "war on pollution" and urban design standards, such as the sponge city programme, among others (Biswas & Hartley 2017). As China's economy settles into a "new normal," an economic model of lower growth rates that also includes greater emphasis on sustainability (Zhang & Chen 2017), increased attention has turned to China's transboundary waters which hold significant potential for increased development, including hydropower production (Feng et al. 2015).

Across the world there are over 300 transboundary watercourses (McCracken & Wolf 2019), with 90% of the global population living in countries with a shared basin (UN Water 2008). China, with the longest land border in the world, shares some 40 major transboundary rivers across 15 transboundary basins (see Figure 1.1), with its 14 neighbouring states, including Afghanistan, Bhutan, India, Kazakhstan, Kyrgyzstan, Laos, Mongolia, Myanmar, Nepal, North Korea, Pakistan, Russia, Tajikistan and Vietnam, and three downstream riparians, including Bangladesh, Cambodia and Thailand. These shared rivers are border rivers, establishing the border between China and its neighbours such as the Heilong-Amur River forming part of the border between China and Russia, successive rivers, those that cross borders such as the Yaluzangbu-Brahmaputra flowing from China to India and Bangladesh, and sometimes both, such as the Lancang-Mekong flowing from China to the delta in Vietnam while also forming parts of the China–Myanmar, Laos–Myanmar and Laos–Thailand border (Biba 2018). Although the characteristics and uses of these rivers and their waters differ from region to region, it is often the case that China is upstream with overall 28 times more water leaving Chinese territory than entering (He 2015).

As an "upstream superpower" (Nickum 2008), China is a geographically, economically and politically important actor in the region and its utilization of transboundary waters will certainly have impacts across Asia and the world. As part of the Hindu-Kush-Himalaya region, for example, many of Asia's great rivers, including the Yangtze, Yellow, Yaluzangbu-Brahmaputra, and the Lancang-Mekong, among others, are entirely within or originate in China. Known as "Asia's Water Tower," the glaciers of this region support 1.7 billion people (CWR 2018: 10). China has sought to further develop the transboundary rivers at its periphery in a variety of ways, most notably through hydropower. These developments are the source of significant tension between China and its neighbours, particularly on its Southwestern

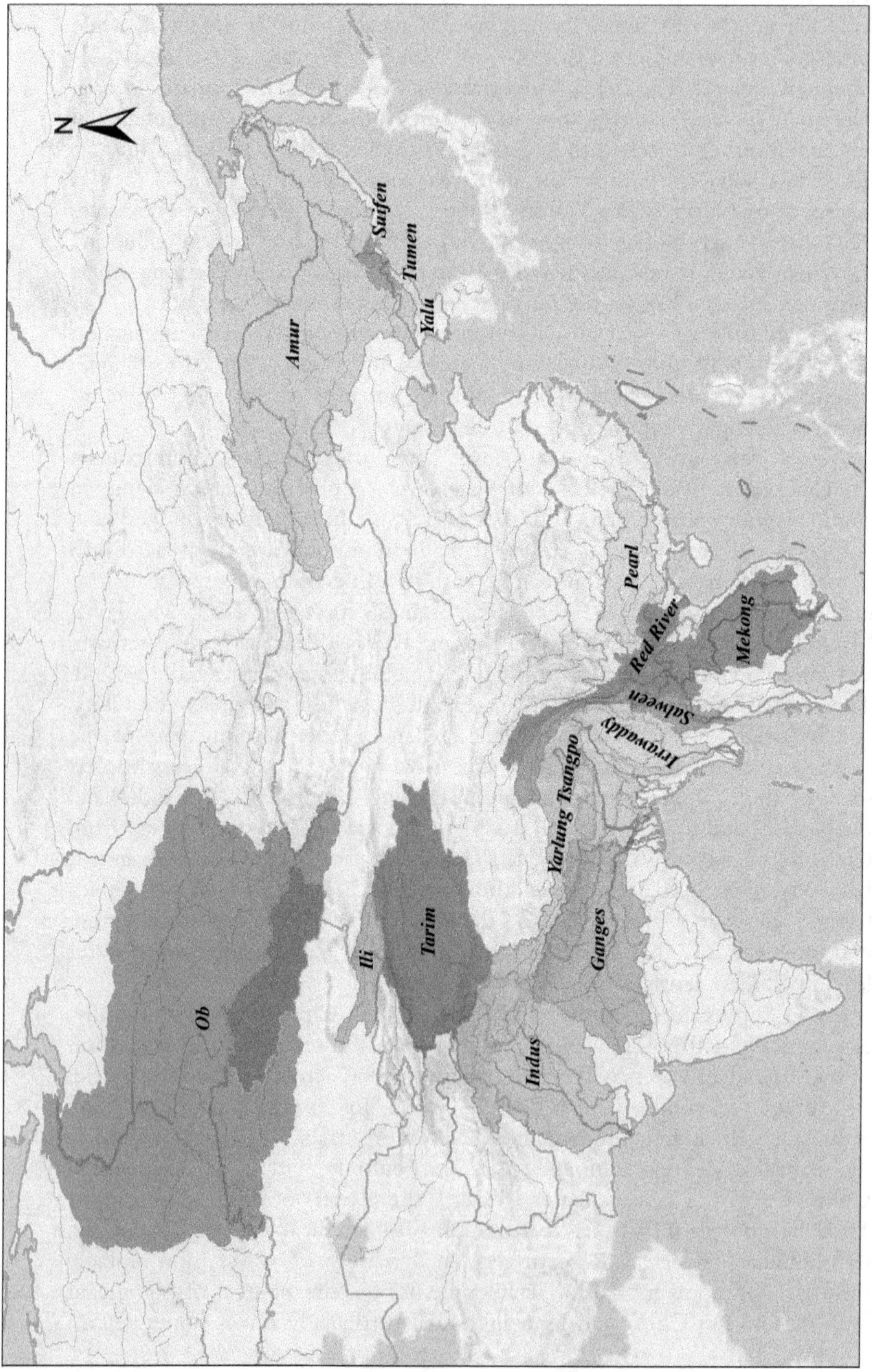

Figure 1.1 Map of China's transboundary basins.

Source: Xie & Jia 2018.

rivers such as the Yaluzangbu-Brahmaputra and Lancang-Mekong. In developing these waters, China faces what Wouters (2014: 71) has referred to as the "upstream dilemma" – how to manage its own water needs while taking into consideration the needs of its downstream neighbours?

It has been argued that water is a "threat multiplier" (ODNI 2014), that conditions of scarcity could contribute to conflict (Homer-Dixon 1994) or even that water scarcity will lead to "water wars" (Chellaney 2013). In regards to transboundary waters, a resource that permanently binds riparians together and must be shared, cooperation, not conflict, is more likely (Bernauer & Böhmelt 2020). China's transboundary waters appear to be no different and we have witnessed a growing trend of cooperation between China and its riparian neighbours. Although law is not a necessary component of cooperation, the conclusion of agreements between states can provide much-needed predictability and stability (Leb 2013; Niv-Solomon 2017). In China's case, this cooperation is guided by over 70 hard and soft-law agreements and related documents signed between China and its riparian neighbours with the aim of jointly governing various aspects of their shared water resources (Devlaeminck et al. 2020).

The need to revisit the law of international watercourses

Across the transboundary basins of the world there are an estimated 3600 agreements related to transboundary freshwaters. Although many of them relate to navigation, over 400 seek to manage the non-navigational uses of international watercourses (Giordano & Wolf 2002). These treaties, however, only cover approximately 60% of the world's transboundary basins (Adeel et al. 2015). Over the past few decades the law of international watercourses has witnessed significant development through the drafting, acceptance and entry into force of the two global water conventions: the 1997 United Nations Convention on the Law of the Non-navigational Uses of International Watercourses (Watercourses Convention) and the 1992 United Nations Economic Commission for Europe (UNECE) Convention on the Protection and Use of Transboundary Watercourses and International Lakes (Water Convention). The Water Convention was drafted by the Working Party of the Senior Advisors to ECE Governments on Environmental and Water Problems alongside input from the UNECE Secretariat in a process beginning in 1990 and concluding with its adoption by UNECE member states in 1992. The Watercourses Convention was first recommended for study by the International Law Commission (ILC) in 1970 with a draft adopted by the United Nations General Assembly (UNGA) in 1997. While the drafting process of the Water Convention was significantly shorter than the Watercourses Convention, taking only two years in comparison to 27, this is likely due to the experience of the UNECE as well as the shared values, norms and history of cooperation between its smaller group of member states.

Although they take slightly different approaches, they are widely regarded as being mutually supportive and synergistic (Tanzi 2015). As framework conventions, the Watercourses Convention and Water Convention are drafted to "provide a framework for later, and more detailed treaties" that are to elaborate upon the principles of the convention (Aust 2000: 97). These frameworks are founded upon the notion of limited territorial sovereignty, the substantive rules of equitable and reasonable utilization and the due diligence obligation not to cause significant harm, both incorporating the duty to cooperate and a series of procedural rules including information sharing, prior notification and consultation. There are, however, slight differences in approach. Whereas the Water Convention has greater emphasis on the prevention of transboundary impact, the Watercourses Convention emphasizes more strongly the importance of allocation via the principle of equitable and reasonable utilization. Despite their differences, they are commonly recognized to "[c]over the same subject-matter and have the same fundamental object and purpose. What one provides for explicitly is often implicit in the other. While their approaches are somewhat different, their normative content is fully compatible" (McCaffrey 2015: 59).

Since their adoption, both the Water Convention and Watercourses Convention have had a significant impact on the governance of transboundary watercourses around the world. Both have now entered into force, with the Water Convention entering into force four years later in 1996, while the Watercourses Convention entered into force 17 years later in 2014. This has certainly not been without challenges, and the Watercourses Convention's entry into force was in no small part due to the efforts of a consortium of actors including international NGOs and scholars across the world (for example, Loures & Rieu-Clarke 2013). As of early 2020, the Watercourses Convention had 37 parties, whereas the Water Convention had 44 (UNTC 1992; 1997). Parties to the global water conventions, particularly the Water Convention which opened for accession globally in 2016, continue to grow, albeit slowly, particularly in Africa where multiple states have expressed their interest in acceding to one or both. In regards to the Water Convention, this is partly attributable to its support from unique mechanisms, including the Meeting of the Parties, Secretariat and innovative Implementation Committee. The global water conventions have had an impact on states even if they are non-parties, as many of the rules and norms they embody are recognized as established customary international law (McCaffrey 2019; McIntyre 2011), a status reflected in their direct and indirect mention in a series of international case law at the ICJ and other bodies, including the *Gabčíkovo-Nagymaros Case* (ICJ 1997), *Pulp Mills Case* (ICJ 2010), *San Juan River Case* (ICJ 2015), the *Indus Waters Kishenganga Arbitration* (Court of Arbitration 2013), and, initiated in 2016, the *Silala Case* (ICJ 2016).

The law of international watercourses itself has witnessed a series of changes as it shifts to take into consideration various concerns of the international community, including a greater focus on the environment, for example, through increased importance of environmental flows and ecosystem services (McIntyre 2019), as well as an increased emphasis on the impact on the human individual, as evidenced through the human right to water which seeks to ensure access to an essential quantity and quality of water (Leb 2012; Winkler 2012). There have even been discussions on the possibility of granting rights to rivers under the law as legal persons (O'Donnell 2018). Much of this action is now being channelled through the Sustainable Development Goals (SDGs), including 17 goals and 169 targets for global development, most importantly SDG 6.5, which aims to implement Integrated Water Resources Management across all scales, including transboundary waters (UNESCO 2018).

Regardless of this progress, challenges lie ahead. Although parties to the global water conventions are growing slowly, there are relatively few in Asia.[1] This is potentially a symptom of a larger issue – a series of misperceptions regarding the global water conventions and the norms of the law of international watercourses. This is particularly the case concerning the centrepiece of the global water conventions, the substantive rules of equitable and reasonable use and the due diligence obligation not to cause significant harm, as evidenced in the voting record of the Watercourses Convention. The Watercourses Convention was adopted by the UNGA in 1997 with 106 votes in favour, 42 abstentions and three votes against.[2] At the time this was hailed as being "adopted by a weighty majority of countries [...] indicating broad agreement in the international community on the general principles governing the non-navigational uses of international watercourses" (McCaffrey & Sinjela 1998: 106). The long period of time before its entry into force and slow adoption by states, however, illustrates that this may not be the case. China, along with Turkey and Burundi, was one of three states that voted against the Convention. Although China did not do so alone, its vote against the Convention has been pointed to as part of arguments that China does not support the norms of the law of international watercourses (Chellaney 2013; Liebman 2005; Menniken 2007). In explanation of its vote, China provided four reasons, including: a lack of consensus; that the Convention did not refer to the sovereignty of watercourse states; opposition to mandatory dispute settlement mechanisms particularly fact-finding being included in a framework convention; and, most interestingly, a perceived imbalance between upstream and downstream states and how these rules would apply to each (UNGA 1997a). China was not alone in its perception that the Convention was imbalanced, and other states, including Colombia, Ethiopia, India, Israel, Rwanda, Slovakia, Spain and Tanzania, also expressed their belief at the time that the Watercourses Convention was imbalanced, applying differently to upstream and downstream countries (UNGA 1997a, 1997b). Subsequent research and analysis of the voting record has confirmed this perception by certain nations, illustrating that downstream states are indeed more likely than upstream states to engage with the Watercourses Convention, supporting the notion that states perceive the Convention and the norms it embodies to be unfair to upstream states (Eckstein 2020; Zhong et al. 2016). Given their similarities, it is likely that such perceptions have dampened support for the Water Convention as well. With these perceptions of the law of international watercourses in the context of the growing importance of transboundary freshwaters, how do we bring all states, upstream and downstream, to come together to cooperate, negotiate new agreements, better implement existing agreements, and to respect and fulfil their obligations under the law of international watercourses?

The lens of reciprocity and outline of the book

In his foundational work on cooperation, Axelrod argued that there are two key ingredients for cooperation to grow and thrive: 1) that cooperation be based on reciprocity, and 2) and that the "shadow of the future," the probability and significance of future cooperation, be of such importance to ensure that this reciprocity is stable (Axelrod 1984: 174). Given that transboundary waters connect states around the world and the absolute importance of water resources to lives and livelihood, it is certainly true that the "shadow of the future" regarding shared water resources is of such a fundamental importance that it provides the motivation for ongoing cooperation. What is unclear, however, is whether this cooperation, when channelled through the frameworks provided by the law of international watercourses, is based upon reciprocity. Reciprocity is closely connected with bilateralism and foundational notions of the international legal system such as sovereign equality, consent and good faith. It has guided states towards cooperation and has acted as the foundation of international legal relations. As described in the *S.S. Cristina*, for example, "each sovereign state within the community of nations accept[s] some subtraction from its full sovereignty in return for similar concessions on the side of the others" (House of Lords 1938: 834).

The predicament that states find themselves in regarding transboundary waters has also been described as a Prisoner's Dilemma (McCaffrey 2019), such that states can cooperate in finding and achieving the best allocation of their shared water resources, or they can defect and utilize them unilaterally as they see fit. If this were a one-time game then it may be in the state's best interest to defect, however, in regards to transboundary waters this is certainly not the case as states will need to repeatedly and jointly approach the issue. The same is true of China who faces the so-called "upstream dilemma," challenged to find a balance between its own interests and needs, and those of its riparian neighbours. Legal agreements can provide the predictability and trust needed to ensure long-lasting, fruitful cooperation, and the law of international watercourses, codified and progressively developed in the Watercourses Convention and Water Convention, offers an engaging legal framework to use in this study on reciprocity.

This book revisits the legal notion of reciprocity with a view to understanding more fully the law and state practice related to transboundary freshwaters, using one of the world's most challenging case studies – China. The book is structured around the key legal elements of transboundary water regimes: scope, substantive rules, procedural rules, institutional mechanisms and dispute settlement (Wouters et al. 2005), each of which will be analysed and interpreted through the lens of reciprocity. In the context of inter-state relations, while it is clear that reciprocity has both political and legal ramifications, this study focuses on the *legal principle* of reciprocity. As such this study is complementary to other studies of China's transboundary waters, which have viewed its practice from the perspective of international relations (for example, Biba 2018; Xie & Jia 2018; Zhang & Li 2018). Clearly, international law requires that we consider the political context of China's transboundary water practice. Nonetheless, the central focus will be on the functioning of the legal norms governing these transboundary waters, considered through treaty and state practice. With international law as a law of cooperation, this analysis will primarily focus on reciprocity as a positive process. Negative reciprocity has been codified in international law via a suite of self-help measures, however even these are a forward-looking actions aiming to re-establish positive cooperation.

After this brief introduction, Chapter 2 aims to explore the emphasis on reciprocity found in China's general approach to international law and transboundary water cooperation. China, with its unique historical and cultural background and experience has developed its approach to international law within this context. Integral to this evolution have been the core principles of national sovereignty and non-interference, as elaborated in the Five Principles of Peaceful Coexistence. The Five Principles have at their core the very notion of reciprocity. This chapter traces the evolution of China's legal cooperation, which is aligned with its approach to international law, anchored in the Five Principles. The chapter then surveys China's treaty practice, specifically considering their "scope" as the first critical element of the transboundary water regime practice.

Chapter 3 explores reciprocity as it contributes to and influences the development of international law. Reciprocity is one factor that leads states to agree to limit their legal claims, a process through which international legal norms and customary international law develop. After examining this process, the chapter discusses this in the context of transboundary waters and its application to the law of international watercourses. This includes a review of the early tension between claims of absolute territorial sovereignty and absolute territorial integrity, exemplified through the *Rio Grande Dispute* between Mexico and the USA, and the *Trail Smelter Case* between the USA and Canada. The reciprocal process that has established limited territorial sovereignty, however, illustrates the true nature of limited territorial sovereignty, not as a claim of altruism, but of enlightened self-interest, providing insight into China's water treaty practice. As the law of international watercourses develops, it has gradually moved towards the establishment of a fourth sovereignty claim, the community of interests, reflected in some ways in China's "community of common destiny."

Chapters 4 and 5 set out to consider the rules codified and progressively developed in the Watercourses Convention, and the Water Convention, and China's state practice regarding its transboundary waters, all through the legal lens of reciprocity. As a legal principle, reciprocity works to ensure fairness and balance in treaties through corresponding rights and duties. After establishing how reciprocity can be utilized as a method of interpretation and its functioning within bilateral and multilateral treaties, Chapter 4 analyses the substantive rules of the law governing the uses of transboundary freshwaters. Founded upon the notion of limited territorial sovereignty, the law of international watercourses has coalesced around two substantive rules: the principle of equitable and reasonable use and the due diligence obligation not to cause significant harm. There has, however, been significant misunderstandings surrounding these two principles, with states often perceiving them to favour either upstream or downstream states. Analysis of these rules through the lens of reciprocity, however, provides greater clarity surrounding rights and duties established by these rules, illustrating that they are capable of promoting balance and fairness through corresponding rights and duties, favouring neither upstream nor downstream states. China has, in many ways, adopted these substantive rules utilizing a similar reciprocal structure. The chapter then turns to explore the impact of the community of interests on these rules, illustrating how bilateralist international law is being "tempered" by such interests (Simma 1989: 844), and how this is reflected in China's own practice, including aspects of human rights and environmental protection. The framework of these rules is complex in bilateral basins, but even more so in multilateral basins. Thus, the chapter concludes with a brief discussion of how institutionalization and benefit-sharing can assist as focal points and strategies to further reciprocity.

This analysis continues in Chapter 5, which focusses on reciprocity's role in cooperation through the procedural rules and dispute settlement mechanisms, provided for in the global water conventions and in the light of China's treaty practice. Reciprocity also contributes to enforcement, playing a strong role in self-help measures of international law, including retorsion, non-performance, suspension and countermeasures, in general international law. In the law of international watercourses, however, these methods of enforcement are rarely resorted to. This chapter thus explores why this may be the case, finding a potential explanation in the possibility of the duty to cooperate as an emerging obligation *erga omnes* that would entail greater restrictions on such measures. As such, states may not be able to rely upon these self-help measures to reinforce cooperation concerning their transboundary waters.

Based on the analysis conducted across the study, the concluding chapter draws together the key observations and sets forth related areas for further study in this field. How might the legal notion of reciprocity contribute to improved transboundary water cooperation? What insights can we make related to China's transboundary water practice? The legal notion of reciprocity, an under-studied concept on the law that governs transboundary freshwater, offers new opportunities for understanding, and, possibly for enhancing improved cooperation and joint management of transboundary waters for China and the world.

Notes

1 Excluding the Middle East, the Watercourses Convention has three parties (Russia, Uzbekistan and Vietnam) and the Water Convention has five (Azerbaijan, Kazakhstan, Russia, Turkmenistan and Uzbekistan) (UNTC 1992, 1997).
2 The original vote had 103 in favour, 3 against (China, Turkey and Burundi), and 22 abstentions. After the vote Belgium, Nigeria and Fiji informed the Secretariat that they wished to vote in favour (UNGA 1997a).

References

Adeel, Z., Aslov, S., Maestu, J. & Unver, O. (2015). *Water Cooperation: Views on Progress and the Way Forward*. Retrieved from http://inweh.unu.edu/portfolio/water-cooperation-views-progress-way-forward/

Aust, A. (2000). *Modern Treaty Law and Practice*. Cambridge/New York: Cambridge University Press.

Axelrod, R. (1984). *The Evolution of Cooperation*. New York: Basic Books Inc.

Badcock, C. (1998). Reciprocity and the Law. *Vermont Law Review*, *22*, 295–303.

Bassiouni, M. C. (1990). A Functional Approach to "General Principles of International Law" *Michigan Journal of International Law*, *11*(2), 768–818.

Bernauer, T. & Böhmelt, T. (2020). International Conflict and Cooperation over Freshwater Resources. *Nature Sustainability*.

Biba, S. (2018). *China's Hydro-Politics in the Mekong: Conflict and Cooperation in Light of Securitization Theory*. Abingdon/New York: Routledge.

Biswas, A. K. & Hartley, K. (2017). China's Groundwater Crisis: Challenges require immediate policy action. *Asia and the Pacific Policy Society*. Retrieved from www.policyforum.net/chinas-groundwater-crisis/

Chellaney, B. (2013). *Water, Peace and War: Confronting the Global Water Crisis*. Lanham: Rowman and Littlefield Press.

Chen, S. (2016). Water Scarcity in China (L. Fan, Trans.). In Y. Zheng & F. Liang (Eds.), *Chinese Research Perspectives on the Environment: Critical Essays on China's Environment and Development* (Vol. 5, pp. 99–116). Leiden and Boston: Brill.

China Daily (2011). Challenges abound as China becomes 2nd largest economy. *China Daily* – February 15. Retrieved from www.chinadaily.com.cn/china/2011-02/15/content_12021239.htm

Chow, D. C. K. & Sheldon, I. (2019). Is Strict Reciprocity Required for Fair Trade?. *Vanderbilt Journal of Transnational Law*, *52*(1), 1–42.

Cotterell, R. (2006). *Law, Culture and Society – Legal Ideas in the Mirror of Social Theory*. Hampshire/Burlington: Ashgate Publishing.

Court of Arbitration (2013). The Indus Waters Kishenganga Arbitration (India & Pakistan) – Final Award (Court of Arbitration December 13, 2013).

Crawford, J. (2012). *Brownlie's Principles of Public International Law* (8 ed.). Oxford: Oxford University Press.

CWR (2018). *No Water No Growth: Does Asia Have Enough Water to Develop?*, China Water Risk. Retrieved from www.chinawaterrisk.org/notices/new-cwr-report-no-water-no-growth/

Devlaeminck, D. J., Wouters, P. & Yang, L. (2020). List of China's Transboundary Water Agreements and Related Documents. *Academia.edu*. Retrieved from https://davidjdevlaeminck.com/research-resources/

Eckstein, G. (2020). The Status of the UN Watercourses Convention: Does it still hold water?. *International Journal of Water Resources Development*, *36*(2–3), 429–61.

Elster, J. (2011). Reciprocity and Norms. In M. Fleurbaey, M. Salles & J. A. Weymark (Eds.), *Social Ethics and Normative Economics: Essays in Honour of Serge-Christophe Kolm* (pp. 327–38). Heidelberg: Springer Publishing.

Escritt, T. & Blenkinsop, P. (2019). Europe's China Ties Must be Reciprocal: Merkel. *Reuters* – March 22. Retrieved from www.reuters.com/article/us-eu-china-germany-idUSKCN1R31TH

ESG (2016). *CEO Briefing: Global Depletion of Aquifers*, Earth Security Group. Retrieved from https://earthsecuritygroup.com/wp-content/uploads/2016/06/ESG-Brief-Aquifers.pdf

Fard, S. N. (2016). *Reciprocity in International Law: Its Impact and Function*. Abingdon/New York: Routledge.

Feng, Y., He, D. & Wang, W. (2015). Identifying China's Transboundary Water Risks and Vulnerabilities – A Multidisciplinary Analysis Using Hydrological Data and Legal/Institutional Settings. *Water International*, *40*(2), 328–41.

Frank, M. R., Obradovich, N., Sun, L., Woon, W. L., LeVeck, B. L. & Rahwan, I. (2018). Detecting Reciprocity at a Global Scale. *Science Advances*, *4*(1).

Giordano, M. A. & Wolf, A. T. (2002). *Atlas of International Freshwater Agreements*. Retrieved from www.transboundarywaters.orst.edu/publications/atlas/

Gouldner, A. W. (1960). The Norm of Reciprocity: A Preliminary Statement. *American Sociological Review*, *25*(2), 161–78.

GWP (2015). *China's Water Resources Management Challenge: The "Three Red Lines."* Global Water Partnership. Retrieved from: www.gwp.org/globalassets/global/toolbox/publications/technical-focus-papers/tfpchina_2015.pdf

He, Y. (2015). China's Practice on the Non-Navigational Uses of Transboundary Waters: Transforming Diplomacy Through Rules Of International Law. *Water International*, *40*(2), 312–27.

Homer-Dixon, T. (1994). Environmental Scarcities and Violent Conflict: Evidence from Cases. *International Security*, *19*(1), 5–40.

House of Lords (1938). The Cristina. *American Journal of International Law* *32*(4), 824–48.

Hutchison, A. (2013). Reciprocity in Contract Law. *Stellenbosch Law Review*, *3*, 3–30.

ICJ (1997). Case Concerning the Gabčíkovo-Nagymaros Project (Hungary v. Slovakia) – Judgement, (International Court of Justice, September 25, 1997).

ICJ (2010). Case Concerning Pulp Mills on the River Uruguay (Argentina v. Uruguay) – Judgement (International Court of Justice, April 20, 2010).

ICJ (2015). Certain Activities Carried out by Nicaragua in the Border Area (Costa Rica v. Nicaragua)/Construction of a Road in Costa Rica Along the San Juan River (Nicaragua v. Costa Rica) – Judgement (International Court of Justice, December 16, 2015).

ICJ (2016). Dispute Over the Status and Use of the Waters of the Silala (Chile v. Bolivia) – Application (International Court of Justice, June 6, 2016).

Kaiman, J. (2013). Chinese environmental official challenged to swim in polluted river. *Guardian* – February 21. Retrieved from www.theguardian.com/environment/2013/feb/21/chinese-official-swim-polluted-river

Kaiman, J. (2014). China says more than half of its groundwater is polluted. *Guardian* – April 23. Retrieved from www.theguardian.com/environment/2014/apr/23/china-half-groundwater-polluted

Kedar, R. D. (2012). Reciprocity in Morality and Law. *Law & Ethics of Human Rights, 6*(2), 203–27.

Keohane, R. O. (1986). Reciprocity in International Relations. *International Organization, 40*(1), 1–27.

Kolm, S. C. (2008). *Reciprocity: An Economics of Social Relations.* Cambridge: Cambridge University Press.

Krystufek, Z. M. (1974). Law and Sociology. *University of Colorado Law Review, 45*, 269–77.

Leb, C. (2012). The Right to Water in a Transboundary Context: Emergence of Seminal Trends. *Water International, 37*(6), 640–53.

Leb, C. (2013). *Cooperation in the Law of Transboundary Water Resources.* Cambridge: Cambridge University Press.

Lenhoff, A. (1956). Reciprocity and the Law of Foreign Judgements: A Historical-Critical Analysis. *Louisiana Law Review, 16*(3), 465–83.

Liebman, A. (2005). Trickle-down Hegemony?: China's "Peaceful Rise" and Dam Building on the Mekong. *Contemporary Southeast Asia: A Journal of Strategic Affairs, 27*(2), 281–304.

Loures, F. R. & Rieu-Clarke, A. (Eds.). (2013). *The UN Watercourses Convention in Force: Strengthening International Law for Transboundary Water Management.* Abingdon/New York: Routledge.

Mazzeschi, R. P. & Viviani, A. (2018). General Principles of International Law: From Rules to Values? In R. P. Mazzeschi & P. D. Sena (Eds.), *Global Justice, Human Rights and the Modernization of International Law* (pp. 113–62). Cham: Springer.

McCaffrey, S. (2015). The 1997 UN Convention: Compatibility and Complementarity. In A. Tanzi, O. McIntyre, A. Kolliopoulos, A. Rieu-Clarke & R. Kinna (Eds.), *The UNECE Convention on the Protection and Use of Transboundary Watercourses and International Lakes: Its Contribution to International Water Cooperation.* Leiden: Brill-Nijhoff.

McCaffrey, S. (2019). *The Law of International Watercourses* (3 ed.). Oxford: Oxford University Press.

McCaffrey, S. & Sinjela, M. (1998). The 1997 United Nations Convention on International Watercourses. *The American Journal of International Law, 92*(1), 97–107.

McCracken, M. & Wolf, A. T. (2019). Updating the Register of International River Basins of the World. *International Journal of Water Resources Development, 35*(5), 732–82.

McIntyre, O. (2011). The World Court's Ongoing Contribution to International Water Law: The Pulp Mills Case between Argentina and Uruguay. *Water Alternatives, 3*(2), 123–44.

McIntyre, O. (2019). Environmental Protection and the Ecosystem Approach. In S. C. McCaffrey, C. Leb & R. T. Denoon (Eds.), *Research Handbook on International Water Law* (pp. 126–46). Cheltenham/Northampton: Edward Elgar.

Menniken, T. (2007). China's Performance in International Resource Politics: Lessons from the Mekong. *Contemporary Southeast Asia: A Journal of Strategic Affairs, 29*(1), 97–120.

Molm, L. D. (2010). The Structure of Reciprocity. *Social Psychology Quarterly, 73*(2), 119–31.

Monaghan, A. (2014). China surpasses US as world's largest trading nation. *Guardian* – January 10. Retrieved from www.theguardian.com/business/2014/jan/10/china-surpasses-us-world-largest-trading-nation

Moore, S. (2013). *Issue Brief: Water Resource Issues, Policy and Politics in China*. The Brookings Institute. Retrieved from www.brookings.edu/research/issue-brief-water-resource-issues-policy-and-politics-in-china/

Nickum, J. E. (2008). The Upstream Superpower: China's International Rivers. In O. Varis, A. Biswas & C. Tortajada (Eds.), *Management of Transboundary Rivers and Lakes* (pp. 227–44), Berlin/Heidelberg: Springer.

Niv-Solomon, A. (2017). *Cooperation and Protracted Conflict in International Affairs: Cycles of Reciprocity*. Cham: Palgrave Macmillan.

O'Donnell, E. (2018). *Legal Rights for Rivers: Competition, Collaboration and Water Governance*. Abingdon/New York: Routledge.

ODNI (2014). *The National Intelligence Strategy of the United States of America*, Office of the Director of National Intelligence. Retrieved from www.dni.gov/files/documents/2014_NIS_Publication.pdf

Orakhelashvili, A. (2019). *Akehurst's Modern Introduction to International Law*. Abingdon/New York: Routledge.

PCIJ (1927). The Case of the S.S. Lotus (The Government of the French Republic v. The Government of the Turkish Republic) (Permanent Court of International Justice, September 7, 1927).

Schneeberger, E. (1949). Reciprocity as a Maxim of International Law. *Georgetown Law Journal, 37*, 29–41.

Simma, B. (1989). Bilateralism and Community Interest in the Law of State Responsibility. In Y. Dinstein & M. Tabory (Eds.), *International Law at a Time of Perplexity* (pp. 821–44). Dordrecht: Martinus Nijhoff.

Simma, B. (2008). Reciprocity. In R. Wolfrum (Ed.), *Max Planck Encyclopedias of International Law*. Oxford: Oxford University Press.

Taekema, S. (2014). Private Law as an Open Legal Order: Understanding Contract and Tort as Interactional Law. *Netherlands Journal of Legal Philosophy, 43*(2), 140–9.

Tanzi, A. (2015). *The Economic Commission for Europe Water Convention and the United Nations Watercourses Convention: An Analysis of their Harmonized Contribution to International Water Law (ECE/MP.WAT/42)*, United Nations Economic Commission for Europe. Retrieved from: www.unwater.org/app/uploads/2017/05/ece_mp.wat_42_eng_web.pdf

Tian, F. & Liu, H. (2016). "China's Water Hegemony in Asia or Shared Rivers, Shared Futures": Which? *Embassy of the People's Republic of China in the Kingdom of Thailand* – July 27. Retrieved from http://th.china-embassy.org/eng/ztbd/t1384905.htm

UNESCO (2018). *Progress on Transboundary Water Cooperation: Global Baseline for SDG Indicator 6.5.2*. United Nations Education, Scientific and Cultural Organization. Retrieved from www.unwater.org/publications/progress-on-transboundary-water-cooperation-652/

UNGA (1997a). *99th Plenary Meeting, Fifty-First Session, United Nations General Assembly*, A/51/PV.99 (May 21, 1997). Retrieved from https://documents-dds-ny.un.org/doc/UNDOC/GEN/N97/855/72/pdf/N9785572.pdf?OpenElement

UNGA (1997b). *Summary Record of the Second Part of the 62nd Meeting, Fifty-First Session, 6th Committee*, A/C.6/51/SR.62/Add.1 (April 4, 1997). Retrieved from https://documents-dds-ny.un.org/doc/UNDOC/GEN/N97/810/90/pdf/N9781090.pdf?OpenElement

UNTC (1992). Convention on the Protection and Use of Transboundary Watercourses and International Lakes: Status. *United Nations Treaty Collection.* Retrieved from https://treaties.un.org/pages/ViewDetails.aspx?src=TREATY&mtdsg_no=XXVII-5&chapter=27&clang=_en

UNTC (1997). Convention on the Law of the Non-Navigational Uses of International Watercourses: Status. *UN Treaty Collection.* Retrieved from https://treaties.un.org/Pages/ViewDetails.aspx?src=TREATY&mtdsg_no=XXVII-12&chapter=27&clang=_en#1

UN Water (2008). *Transboundary Waters: Sharing Benefits, Sharing Responsibilities.* UN Water. Retrieved from www.unwater.org/publications/transboundary-waters-sharing-benefits-sharing-responsibilities/

VornDick, W. (2015). Why climate change could be China's biggest security threat. *The Diplomat* – August 14. Retrieved from http://thediplomat.com/2015/08/why-climate-change-could-be-chinas-biggest-security-threat/

Water Convention (1992). Convention on the Protection and Use of Transboundary Watercourses and International Lakes (adopted on March 17, 1992; entered into force October 6, 1996).

Watercourses Convention (1997). United Nations Convention on the Law of Non-Navigational Uses of International Watercourses (adopted on May 21, 1997; entered into force August 17, 2014).

Westerman, P. (2014). Reciprocity: A Fragile Equilibrium. *Netherlands Journal of Legal Philosophy*, *43*(2), 172–184.

Winkler, I. T. (2012). *The Human Right to Water: Significant, Legal Status and Implications for Water Allocation.* Oxford/Portland: Hart Publishing.

Wouters, P. (2014). The Yin and Yang of International Water Law: China's Transboundary Water Practice and the Changing Contours of Sovereignty *RECIEL*, *23*(1), 67–75.

Wouters, P. K., Vinogradov, S., Allan, A., Jones, P. & Rieu-Clarke, A. (2005). *Sharing Transboundary Waters: An Integrated Assessment of Equitable Entitlement – The Legal Assessment Model.* Paris: UNESCO. Retrieved from www.gwp.org/globalassets/global/gwp-cacena_files/en/pdf/legal_model_doc.pdf

Xie, L. & Jia, S. (2018). *China's International Transboundary Rivers: Politics, Security and Diplomacy of Shared Water Resources.* Abingdon/New York: Routledge.

Zhang, J. & Chen, J. (2017). Introduction to China's New Normal Economy. *Journal of Chinese Economic and Business Studies*, *15*(1), 1–4.

Zhang, H. & Li, M. (Eds.). (2018). *China and Transboundary Water Politics in Asia.* Abingdon/New York: Routledge.

Zhong, Y., Tian, F., Hu, H., Grey, D. & Gilmont, M. (2016). Rivers and Reciprocity: Perceptions and Policy on International Watercourses. *Water Policy*, *18*(3), 803–25.

Zimmerman, A., Tomuschat, C., Oellers-Frahm, K. & Tams, C. (2012). *The Statute of the International Court of Justice: A Commentary.* Oxford: Oxford University Press.

2 Reciprocity in China's international legal relations and transboundary waters

Alongside its rise, China has taken a more prominent role on the global stage, as a member of various multilateral institutions such as the World Trade Organization and International Monetary Fund, a permanent member on the UN Security Council where it wields the power of the veto, member of various regional organizations such as Association of Southeast Asian Nations, and has even established its own multilateral institutions including the Shanghai Cooperation Organization and Asian Infrastructure Investment Bank. To actualize its "peaceful rise", enact its good neighbour policy, and often as part of its membership in the aforementioned institutions, China has signed approximately 23,000 bilateral agreements and over 400 multilateral agreements (Burnay 2018). China's engagement with the international order, however, has often been viewed with scepticism, with some even accusing China of being "revisionist" seeking to change the world order (Zhao 2018). While China is "unlikely to become a model of compliance" (deLisle 2000: 275) and, like many other powerful states, will consider violating international law when it is in its interest to do so, it also does not appear to be a disruptive force (Burnay 2018; Saul 2019).[1] Whereas it is certainly true that China's attitude towards international law is not uniform across all subject areas, it "at least at a high level of abstraction, does not appear to vary significantly from those of other major powers" (Cohen 2019: 161). Like states around the world, a major component of China's approach to international law and state relations is the fundamental principle of reciprocity which works in various ways in China's international agreements. Although these agreements cover a wide variety of issue areas (see Table 2.1), reciprocity is arguably present in all of them, from economic law which "provide[s] for reciprocal rights and obligations among states" (Petersmann 2012: 121); humanitarian law regimes which have "long been conditioned on notions of reciprocal obligations and observations" (Watts 2009: 368); to human rights agreements which, "cannot be based on reciprocity since their aim is to protect the rights of relatively powerless individuals who cannot reciprocate against a powerful state" (Fard 2016: 58), yet still reflect some aspects of reciprocity as a reciprocal promise (Simma 2008). China has most explicitly emphasized reciprocity through the Five Principles of Peaceful Coexistence, originally adopted in 1954 by China and India (China–India 1954). These principles, founded upon "mutual respect for each other's territorial integrity and sovereignty," remain prevalent in China's international law discourse and treaty practice.

A similar trend can be seen on China's transboundary waters. Whereas previously China seemed willing to go it alone in developing its transboundary waters, most notably through upstream hydropower development, after a period of time and series of events it appears to have, in some ways, shifted tactics. In recognition of its responsibilities, potential impact on its neighbours and relations at its periphery, China has since established cooperative relations guided by a series of bilateral agreements, alongside other related documents, with its riparian neighbours. Working from the basic definition of reciprocity offered in Chapter 1, an *exchange* that is *contingent* and roughly *equivalent*, this chapter first aims to trace the development of China's modern reciprocal approach to international law via the Five Principles, beginning with an historic analysis, highlighting how China's historic relation with international law has fostered a strong emphasis on state sovereignty and equality in China's modern approach to international law. This notion of sovereignty, however, is not absolute but shaped and formed through reciprocal norms found in the Five Principles. Such an approach to state relations and international law permeates China's transboundary water cooperation, evidenced by the principles of cooperation found in the preamble as well as the scope of its legal agreements. The preamble of an agreement is a section at the beginning of a legal document that "defines, in general terms, the purposes and considerations that led the parties to conclude the treaty" (Mbengue 2006: para. 1). The issue of scope is of fundamental importance to international law generally, and the law of international watercourse specifically, where it determines the legal reach of a treaty, referring to the waters the treaty relates to, who the parties are, and how the body of water is defined (Wouters 2013). For China, the question of scope is a question of sovereignty, as it determines the extent to which China must take its neighbours into consideration (Wouters & Chen 2013). The preamble and scope thus have a significant impact on the application of reciprocity in transboundary water treaties, helping us to determine the extent of and potential units of legal exchange and the actors involved. Thus, the chapter offers an analysis of the scope of China's legal agreements, and, in instances where legal agreements are few, the general scope of China's transboundary water cooperation. In doing so, this chapter aims to illustrate that China's reciprocal approach to international law is evident on its transboundary waters, apparent through the influence of the Five Principles in China's transboundary water relations and treaty practice.

Table 2.1 A selection of multilateral treaties that China is party to

Treaty	*Date of entry into force for China*
1947 General Agreement on Tariffs and Trade	2001-12-11
1948 Convention on the Prevention and Punishment of the Crime of Genocide	1983-04-18
1951 Convention Relating to the Status of Refugees	1982-09-24
1961 Vienna Convention on Diplomatic Relations	1975-11-25
1965 Agreement Establishing the Asian Development Bank	1986-03-10
1966 International Covenant on Economic, Social and Cultural Rights	2001-03-27
1969 Vienna Convention on the Law of Treaties	1997-09-03
1971 Convention on Wetlands of International Importance Especially as Waterfowl Habitat	1992-07-31
1982 UN Convention on the Law of the Sea	1996-07-07
1987 Montreal Protocol on Substances that Deplete the Ozone Layer	1991-06-14
1989 Convention on the Rights of the Child	1992-04-02
1992 Convention on Biological Diversity	1993-01-05
1992 Convention on the Prohibition of the Development, Production, Stockpiling and Use of Chemical Weapons and on their Destruction	1997-04-25
1992 UN Framework Convention on Climate Change	1993-01-05
1997 Kyoto Protocol to the UN Framework Convention on Climate Change	2002-08-30
2015 Paris Agreement	2016-09-03

Source: UNTC 2020.

China's reciprocal approach to state relations and international law

Reciprocity acts as one of the foundations of modern Chinese society, evident in business relations (Westwood et al. 2004), family structures (Schwarz et al. 2010; Zhang et al. 2014), social relations (Chen & Chen 2004) and prevalent in various aspects of Confucianism (Csikszentmihalyi 2008). With reciprocity engrained in Chinese society, as it is in societies around the world, it is not surprising that it has taken on a prominent role in China's modern perspective and approach to international law. China's perspectives on international law can be traced back to Confucian philosophy and the concepts of *Li* and *Fa*, where *Li* represents the moral rules that regulate society, and *Fa* represents the legal framework, closely linked to punishment (Pan 2011). From a traditional Chinese perspective, "international *Li*," or international law, operated like a hierarchical family relationship, and did not include notions of sovereignty and independence (Pan 2011: 235). This is apparent in the tribute system, common in state relations of Imperial

China, in which China received tribute from neighbouring states. This system had hints of reciprocity as states and their rulers would give up part of their sovereignty in exchange for assistance in maintaining their rule, whereas China ensured, for example, secure and peaceful borders (Lam 1968). This emphasis on reciprocity between China and its neighbours appears to have spilt over into various policies of Imperial China, including the border control system (Edwards 1987).

After the Opium Wars (1839–42) China was forced to sign a series of unequal treaties, treaties that, although not necessarily invalid (Peters 2007),[2] are imbalanced in the sense that parties "do not reciprocally promise to each other the same things, or things equivalent" (Vattel 2008: 349). These unequal treaties required China to cede Hong Kong, Taiwan and the Shandong Peninsula to the United Kingdom, Japan and Germany respectively, while large swaths of land were ceded to Russia via treaty under the threat of military force (Chen 2013; Xue 2005). Such actions were justified by Western powers at the time as China did not consider state sovereignty to be a principle of international law (Chan 2015). After the founding of the first republic in 1911, China experienced a series of civil wars, internal discontent and Japanese aggression (Xue 2005). At the breakout of World War I, Japan took control of Shandong province claiming that it was German territory, and their control over Shandong was confirmed after the war in the Treaty of Versailles (Chan 2015). With the founding of the People's Republic of China in 1949, China reviewed all foreign treaties concluded by previous governments to determine whether they should be annulled, amended, replaced or recognized (Xue 2005), and it is around this time that China's strong support for the notion of sovereignty and mutual respect began to take form.

Sovereignty, a foundational notion of international law, has both internal and external aspects. Internally, sovereignty implies the power of the state to regulate its territory and the persons, people and things within it. Externally, however, sovereignty implies an independence from outside interference (Wang 1990). Throughout its development, China has remained a strong supporter of both internal and external sovereignty, through which it rejects interference in its own sovereignty as well as interference in the sovereignty of other states (Burnay 2018). Besides protecting its internal affairs, however, China views sovereignty as "a claim about the way in which how different political and social systems, different forms of civilization and culture should correlate and treat each other in international relations" (Xue 2011: 106). This view of sovereignty and the way states should conduct their relations is most evident in the Five Principles of Peaceful Coexistence, first adopted in 1954 by China and India (China–India 1954). These principles have shaped Chinese foreign relations, and include:

1) Mutual respect for each other's territorial integrity and sovereignty,
2) Mutual non-aggression,

3) Mutual non-interference in each other's internal affairs,
4) Equality and mutual benefit, and
5) Peaceful co-existence.

(China–India 1954)

They have since appeared in various documents, expanded upon in the Ten Principles of Bandung of the 1955 Bandung Conference (Wang 1990), evident in the 1970 Declaration on Principles of International Law concerning Friendly Relations and Cooperation among States (UNGA 1970) as well as the 1972 China–USA Shanghai Communiqué (China–USA 1972), and affirmed in China's Constitution (PRC 1982). Given their mutuality, reciprocity lies at the core of these principles (Cohen 1973; Jia 2019), and with their foundation in state sovereignty and equality (Xue 2007) they echo the principles of the UN Charter. In the international legal context interpreted through the lens of reciprocity as a contingent and proportional exchange, mutual non-aggression, for example, would imply that positively all states are obligated not to use force and that negatively any use of force could be met with a reciprocal proportionate use of force. This closely resembles the UN Charter prohibition on the use of force and right to self-defence (UN Charter 1945: art. 2(4) & 51). As a framework for cooperation and establishing peaceful state relations each of these principles are reciprocal in a positive way, however, not all of the Five Principles have negative reciprocal aspects. For example, although it is certainly the case that states should reciprocally respect each other's territorial integrity and sovereignty, it is certainly not the case that if a state were to infringe upon a state's territorial integrity or sovereignty that this would permit the other to reciprocate in kind and violate that state's territorial integrity or sovereignty. In the UN Charter this resembles the strong emphasis on the principle of sovereign equality, and, given the *jus cogens* nature of this norm, the prohibition on the use of force and the requirement for states to settle their disputes through peaceful means (UN Charter 1945: art. 2(1), 2(3) & 2(4)).

At the end of the Cultural Revolution in 1976, China began its policy of economic reform and opening up and Chinese society underwent a series of social and institutional changes (Chan 2015). It is at this time that China began to view international law as a tool, "an effective method for integrating China into international society for economic benefit" (Pan 2011: 239). Its view of international law and state relations as such, however, continued to be based upon the Five Principles (Xue 2007), which China reaffirmed on the 60th anniversary of the Bandung Conference (Xi 2015a, 2015b). Reflecting a reciprocal approach to international law, China has even stated that it considers the Five Principles to be "basic principles of international law" (Xi 2014). The establishment of treaties, described as "maids-of-all-work in international law" (Orakhelashvili 2019: 33), is one of the "oldest and most characteristic exercises of independence or sovereignty on the part of States" (McNair 1986: 36). Their establishment is founded upon the notion of sovereign equality under the law, similar to the notion of mutual respect for sovereignty in the Five Principles. As a legal principle reciprocity is considered to be the foundation of international law, but it is not as equally influential across all areas of international law. China's emphasis on reciprocity, however, appears across its engagement with international law, in areas that are both heavily and minimally influenced by the legal principle, as exemplified in its engagement with the economic law regime and climate change regime.

China's engagement with international law has been most apparent in regards to the international economic law regime. As China has opened up over the past few decades, it has established multiple Free Trade Agreements and over 140 Bilateral Investment Treaties (UNCTAD 2020), often themselves called "Agreements for the Promotion of Reciprocal Protection of Investment" (For example, Canada–China 2012; China–Italy 1985), with partner countries across the world. These agreements, and international economic law generally, are based upon reciprocal rights and duties between parties, for example, in trade agreements which provides reciprocal rights and duties concerning market access between parties (Matsushita et al. 2017). Most notable, however, is China's 2001 accession to the World Trade Organization (WTO). As part of its accession, China was required to become party to a series of reciprocal agreements, "constitut[ing] a promise to each and every WTO member individually" (Pauwelyn 2003: 69). Whereas the negotiation process and agreement that China signed to become a member has been described as including "nearly no reciprocal trade openings" and with concern that China became "a formal yet less-than equal member of the world trading system" (Wu 2011: 244), in state comments prior to accession it recognized the reciprocal nature of its WTO obligations (WTO 2001a) and that the significant benefits for both China and the world that arise from conceding on various trade issues would incentivize China's compliance (WTO 2001b). This highlights that the benefits China expected to receive were proportionate, or perhaps even greater than the sovereignty it conceded regarding trade issues.

Not all agreements or provisions, however, are based upon reciprocity but instead require states to accept obligations of conduct within their own territory. They therefore do not necessarily establish rights and obligations based upon reciprocity between states, but to the international community (Bodansky 2010; Brunée 1989). Often found in, but not limited to, the field of environmental law, these agreements do not necessarily reflect reciprocity, but are "built on reciprocity" supported by the community's reciprocal, collective interest in the enforcement of treaty obligations and the confidence each party has to the fulfilment of the obligations by the other parties (Bodansky 2010: 226; Brunée 1989). China has engaged with a series of environmental regimes concerning issues such as desertification, biodiversity, and, most notably, climate change. Although China's participation in climate change negotiations has not always been viewed in a positive light (Dimitrov 2010), it has been particularly active in the climate change regime, especially recently as calls for China to take a leadership role have grown. China was a strong advocate for the notion of "common but differentiated responsibilities" of developing countries which recognizes that climate change will have a common impact on all states but that each state's responsibility for this is different and that not all should contribute equally to resolving the issue (Stone 2004). Found in Article 3 of the United Nations Framework Convention on Climate Change (UNFCCC 1992) and Article 10 of the Kyoto Protocol (1997), this reflects the common reciprocal interest of states to mitigate climate change while establishing a non-reciprocal obligation as states will take individual action within their own territory to do so. While the legal obligation is non-reciprocal, when viewed in light of reciprocity and the greater context of the negotiations it is ultimately a question of the rough equivalence of their actions, with China's strong support for the principle indicating it believed that it should receive the benefits from climate mitigation in exchange for less than what others may contribute. As it became more difficult to argue that they are a developing country and as emissions have increased (Shen & Xie 2019), China has taken on a more central role in the fight against climate change and both the international law related to climate change and China's engagement with it have increased in their emphasis on reciprocity. States around the world were cautious regarding Chinese action on climate change, fearing that they would be placed at a disadvantage if they were to act without China (Leggett et al. 2008), and wished for reciprocal commitments (Stroik et al. 2019; Tvinnereim et al. 2016). Unlike its predecessors, the Paris Agreement obligates states to individually determine their national contributions. Although reciprocity is not explicitly mentioned, these individually determined state contributions can act as a reciprocal challenge for others to do more (Bernauer et al. 2016; Falkner 2016; Keohane & Victor 2016). In the leadup to the Paris Agreement, China and the USA sought to reciprocally challenge each other, committing to cooperation on climate change and various contributions (China–USA 2014), ultimately ensuring that both countries are disadvantaged. This was repeated in 2015 and 2016 (China–USA 2015, 2016), establishing a solid foundation for the Paris Agreement and nationally determined contributions (Shen & Xie 2019). However, as the USA reassesses its international relationships with strict reciprocity in mind, it has since pulled out of the Paris Agreement. China has since reaffirmed its commitment to the Agreement and appears to be on track to meet its national contributions (Gabbatiss 2019; Pennetier 2019). Whether its climate commitments continue to challenge other states to do more, however, remains to be seen.

The foundation and scope of China's transboundary water cooperation

China's transboundary water relations fall in line with its approach to international law, emphasizing reciprocity and sovereignty over its transboundary water resources. This reciprocal approach is illustrated in both the preamble and scope of its transboundary water agreements. Although it does not often establish rights and obligations, the preamble at the beginning of an agreement assists with interpretation, can help to identify the aims, object and purpose of the treaty, reflect the context of the establishment of the treaty, and, in some cases, "come very close to being legislative in nature" (Klabbers 2018: 182). The scope of an international agreement, often found in the first few provisions, is a fundamental aspect of a treaty, identifying its legal reach. In regards to international watercourses, scope assists in determining "to what extent a riparian State should bear the legal duty to give due consideration to the interests of other riparian States and restrict its rights to use the water resources within its own territory" (Xue 1992: 55). Thus, the question of scope is not solely a question of the geographical dynamics of a region (however they will certainly play a role), but a question of international law (Wouters & Chen 2013) and, when states are determining that scope, of their approach to international law. In terms of reciprocity, the preamble acts as the basic foundation of the legal relationship, telling us the drafting and interpretive context of that agreement. The scope goes on to indicate which parties will conduct a reciprocal exchange, and the potential units of that exchange. In other words, it tells us "how to reconcile the relation between the natural phenomenon of interconnected physical unity of international watercourses and the social phenomenon of independent riparian sovereignty rights over territorial water resources" (Xue 1992: 46), one being a geographical construct and the other being a social construct influenced by reciprocity.

The preambles and scope of the 1997 United Nations Convention on the Law of the Non-navigational Uses of International Watercourses (Watercourses Convention) and the 1992 United Nations Economic Commission for Europe (UNECE) Convention on the Protection and Use of Transboundary Watercourses and International Lakes (Water Convention) are similar in their approach. Their preambles provide the context of their drafting and overall aims to be achieved; however, neither the preamble of the Watercourses Convention nor Water Convention mentions reciprocity or similar norms. They do, however, emphasize the need for and importance of cooperation (Water Convention 1992: preamble; Watercourses Convention 1997: preamble). The Water Convention applies to transboundary waters as "any surface or ground waters which mark, cross or are located on boundaries between two or more States" (Water Convention 1992: art. 1(1)). The Watercourses Convention applies specifically to "uses of international watercourses and of their waters for purposes other than navigation," defining a "watercourse" as a "system of surface waters and groundwaters constituting by virtue of their physical relationship a unitary whole and normally flowing into a common terminus" (Watercourses Convention 1997: art. 1(1) & 2(a)). A watercourse is transboundary when parts of that watercourses are found in two or more states (Watercourses Convention 1997: art. 2(b)). Reflecting its overall approach to international law and state sovereignty, China voted against the Watercourses Convention citing four reasons, one of which was that a state "enjoys indisputable territorial sovereignty over those parts of international watercourses that flows through its territory" (UNGA 1997), echoing the first of the Five Principles and providing support for the notion that the scope of the global water conventions directly relates to a state's sovereignty.

China's transboundary waters can be divided into three areas: the Northeast, Northwest and Southwest (Feng et al. 2015; He et al. 2014; Xie & Jia 2018). Cooperation is most developed in the Northeast and Northwest governed by multiple treaties, and it is developing incrementally in the Southwest where legally binding documents are limited. China prefers a "one country, one treaty" approach (Chen et al. 2013: 219), and its treaties are therefore primarily bilateral (see Table 2.2). Many of these bilateral agreements focus on technical issues, such as information sharing (Wouters & Chen 2013). There are instances of multilateral cooperation (see Table 2.3), but they are often broad in scope, focussing on water issues alongside a variety of other concerns.

Legal cooperation is most developed in the Northeast and Northwest. In the Northeast, China shares rivers with Russia, Mongolia and North Korea. Regarding the major rivers, China is upstream on the Yalu River (North Korea), Tumen River (North Korea and Russia), and the Suifen River (Russia), but neither downstream or upstream on the Heilong-Amur River (Mongolia and Russia) which forms a large portion of the border between China and Russia.[3] In the Northwest, China shares rivers with Kazakhstan, Kyrgyzstan, as well as Mongolia and Russia, where it is primarily upstream, for example, on the Irtysh River (Kazakhstan, Mongolia and Russia), Ili (Kazakhstan and Kyrgyzstan) and the Tarim River (Kyrgyzstan) (Xie & Jia 2018). There are a series of (mostly) bilateral agreements through which China and its neighbours govern these transboundary waters, reflecting the Five Principles, reciprocity and sovereignty. The preamble of the 1962 China–Mongolia Boundary Treaty, for example, explicitly recognizes the reciprocal aspects of their legal cooperation as the border delimitation was completed "in accordance with the principles of mutual respect, equality and reciprocal advantage, mutual understanding and reciprocal concessions, through friendly consultations" so as to benefit the peoples of both countries (China–Mongolia 1962: preamble). This heavily reflects the Five Principles, with similar norms found in the 2001 China–Kazakhstan Agreement on Cooperation in the Use and Protection of Transboundary Rivers, which explicitly includes and expands upon the Five Principles as it is governed by "mutual respect for independence, sovereignty, and territorial integrity, non-interference in each other's internal affairs, equality and mutual benefit, and peaceful coexistence, in a spirit of mutual understanding, mutual amenability, and friendly consultation" (China–Kazakhstan 2001: preamble). The 1994 China–Mongolia Agreement on Protection and Utilization of Boundary Waters does not explicitly mention reciprocity; however, it is aimed at "developing good-neighbourly relations and cooperation […] on the basis of equality and mutual benefit" (China–Mongolia 1994: preamble).

Table 2.2 A selection of China's bilateral transboundary water treaties and related documents

Party		*Agreement*
Bangladesh	2008	Memorandum of Understanding Concerning the Provision of Hydrological Information of the Yaluzangbu-Brahmaputra River in Flood Season by China to Bangladesh
Bhutan	2008	Memorandum of Understanding upon Provision of Hydrological Information of the Yaluzangbu-Brahmaputra in the Flood Season
Cambodia	2016	Memorandum of Understanding on the Study of Master Plan on Water Resources Planning Projects, Arrangement of Disciplinary Systems and Support Facilities of International Water Resources Projects
India	2013	Memorandum of Understanding on Strengthening Cooperation on Trans-border Rivers
	2005	Memorandum of Understanding on the Provision of Hydrological Data on Langqen Zangbo-Sutlej during Flood Season
	2002	Memorandum of Understanding on the Sharing of Hydrological Information on the Yaluzangbu-Brahmaputra River during the Flood Season (renewed in 2008, 2013 & 2018)
Kazakhstan	2011	Agreement on Protection of Water Quality of Transboundary Rivers
	2006	Agreement on Exchange of Hydrological and Hydro-chemical Information (Data) of Border Gauging Stations on Major Transboundary Rivers
	2001	Agreement on Cooperation in the Use and Protection of Transboundary Rivers
Laos	2014	Memorandum of Understanding in the Field of Water Resources Cooperation
	1993	Treaty on the Border System
Mekong River Commission	2002	Agreement on Provision of Hydrological Information on the Lancang-Mekong River during Flood Season (Renewed in 2008, 2013 & 2019)
Mongolia	2010	Treaty on the Management of the Boundary
	1994	Agreement on Protection and Utilization of Boundary Waters
	1962	Boundary Treaty
Myanmar	1997	Agreement on Border Management and Cooperation
	1997	Agreement on Freight and Passenger Transport along the Lancang-Mekong River
North Korea	2002	The Protocol on Cooperation on Navigation and Shipping in Boundary Rivers
	1964	The Protocol on Borderline
	1962	The Treaty on Borderline
Russia	2008	Agreement on Management and Protection of Transboundary Waters
	2001	Treaty of Good-Neighborliness and Friendly Cooperation
Vietnam	2009	Land Border Management System Agreement
	1991	Provisional Agreement on the Settlement of Border Affairs

Note

* For a complete, and regularly updated list of China's transboundary water treaties, see Devlaeminck et al. 2020.

The scope of these agreements varies, becoming broader over time (Su 2014). The 1994 China–Mongolia Agreement applies to the listed transboundary waters (Halaha River, Kerulen River, Bor Nor Lake and Bulgan River) and any other "lakes, rivers, streams and other water that straddle or rest on the boundary line between the two countries" (China–Mongolia 1994: art. 1). Although the use of the term "boundary" does not recognize the flow of the water as it crosses the border (Su 2014: 4), it does emphasize the sovereignty of the parties. Later agreements have become broader in scope, but are still narrower than the Watercourses Convention. More closely resembling the Water Convention and its use of the term "transboundary waters," the 2008 China–Russia Agreement applies to "the protection and utilization of transboundary waters," referring to "any rivers, lakes, streams or swamps that straddle or rest on the boundary line between the two states" (Su 2014: 4). Similarly, the 2001 China–Kazakhstan Agreement applies to "transboundary river[s]," meaning "all rivers and river flows that cross state borders or are located along the border [...]" (China–Kazakhstan 2001: art. 1). In the Northeast on the Tumen River, China, the Democratic People's Republic of Korea, Mongolia and Russia came together to sign the 1994 Agreement on the Establishment of the Tumen River Area Development Coordination. This multilateral, regional initiative covers a wide range of issue areas, aiming to improve regional "transport, trade, investment, energy, tourism and environmental protection of the river" (Lee et al. 2019: 22). In order "to strengthen economic and technical cooperation and to attain greater growth and sustainable development," the states will "implement this agreement on the basis of the sovereignty and independence of all states, equality, mutual benefit and good neighbourliness" (Tumen 1994: art. 1(1–2)).

Table 2.3 A selection of China's multilateral transboundary water treaties and related documents

Parties (other than China)	*Agreement*	
Laos, Myanmar, Thailand	2000	Agreement on Commercial Navigation on Lancang/Mekong River
	2011	Joint Statement on Law Enforcement Cooperation along the Mekong River
North Korea, Mongolia, Russia, South Korea	1994	Agreement on the Establishment of the Consultative Commission for the Development of the Tumen River Economic Development Area and Northeast Asia
	1994	Memorandum of Understanding on Environmental Principles Governing the Tumen River Economic Development Area and Northeast Asia

Note

* For a complete, and regularly updated list of China's transboundary water treaties, see Devlaeminck et al. 2020.

In the Southwest, legal cooperation is growing, supplemented by a series of Chinese-led initiatives with a broad scope. It is also in this region where the emphasis on the Five Principles and reciprocity is most explicit. Many of the rivers of this region originate in China, including the Ganges River (Bangladesh, India and Nepal), Irrawaddy (Myanmar), Nu-Salween River (Myanmar and Thailand), Lancang-Mekong River (Cambodia, Laos, Myanmar, Thailand and Vietnam), Sengezangmu-Indus River (Afghanistan, India and Pakistan), Yaluzangbu-Brahmaputra (Bangladesh, Bhutan and India) and the Yuan-Red (Vietnam) (Xie & Jia 2018). Levels of legal cooperation in the region vary, often dependent on past levels of general engagement between China and its neighbours (Ho 2014). These relations are under increasing strain as China has developed upstream hydropower on both the Yaluzangbu-Brahmaputra and Lancang-Mekong. China has already constructed at least one hydropower dam on the Yaluzangbu-Brahmaputra, with at least three more planned (Yasuda et al. 2017). On the Lancang-Mekong, China has constructed a cascade of hydropower dams, including 11 dams in operation and three in the planning stages (Eyler & Weatherby 2020). Recent studies have illustrated that these upstream hydropower dams have had some impact on downstream states, a point of serious concern (for example, Basist & Williams 2020; MRC 2017, 2019; Räsänen et al. 2017).

In spite of these difficulties, cooperation in the region has developed incrementally. China and India have established cooperation via a series of joint statements and MoUs, and, given ongoing border issues, this is largely based upon the Five Principles. For example, in the 2003 Declaration on Principles for Relations and Comprehensive Cooperation the two states reaffirm that their relationship is conducted "on the basis of the Five Principles of Peaceful Coexistence, mutual respect and sensitivity for each other's concerns and equality" (China–India 2003). Water cooperation on the Yaluzangbu-Brahmaputra is limited to a handful of agreements and pledges with limited scope, primarily to share information during the flood season. The Five Principles are not explicit within the preamble of these information-sharing agreements; however, the context of this information sharing illustrates that it is dependent on reciprocity and mutual respect for sovereignty. For example, information sharing on the Yaluzangbu-Brahmaputra River was paused during the 2017 military tension in Doklam, after Chinese troops began the construction of a road in territory disputed by China and Bhutan. Indian troops responded, resulting in a 73-day standoff between Chinese and Indian forces (Panda 2017). During this time, hydrological information sharing between China and India stopped, as China claimed that the hydrological station was being upgraded (Gupta 2018; PTI 2017). Experts on both sides, however, speculate that this was related to the tension at Doklam (Ho et al. 2019), with some even going so far as to say that this was a reciprocal response to a violation of Chinese sovereignty (Zhao 2017).

The lower Mekong states (Cambodia, Laos, Thailand and Vietnam) came together in 1995 to sign the Agreement on the Cooperation for the Sustainable Development of the Mekong River, establishing the Mekong River Commission (MRC). China, however, has chosen not to join, instead becoming an observer to the Commission. This does not mean that there is no cooperation between China and the Mekong sates, as China and the MRC signed the 2002 Agreement on Provision of Hydrological Information on the Lancang/Mekong River during the Flood Season, renewed in 2008, 2013 and 2019 (MRC 2002, 2008, 2013, 2019). The preamble of this agreement mentions "existing friendly relations and traditional cooperation," without reference to reciprocity or reciprocal norms. The agreement is very narrow in scope, specifically concerned with information sharing from select sites in Chinese territory at the indicated times of year (MRC 2002). In order to counter mounting criticism concerning China's upstream hydropower development, establish a higher level of control and leadership in the region, increase institutional capacity and development and complement its Belt and Road Initiative (Biba 2018), in 2015 China and its downstream neighbours launched the Lancang-Mekong Cooperation (LMC) Mechanism. The LMC is one of only two regional mechanisms that involve all riparians, the other being the Greater Mekong Subregion. Although the LMC and its related documents (see Table 2.4) do not amount to a water-sharing agreement and their legal status is unclear, they are based upon the notion of reciprocity, offering a broad scope. Cooperation under the LMC is conducted on the basis of "consensus, equality, mutual consultation and coordination, voluntarism, common contribution and shared benefits" as well as a respect for the UN Charter and international law (LMC 2016: preamble). The scope of the LMC Mechanism is broad, taking a "3+5" approach involving three pillars (political and security issues, economy and sustainable development and people-to-people exchange) and five cooperation areas (connectivity, production capacity, cross-border economic cooperation, agriculture, poverty reduction and *water resources*) (LMC 2016). This framework was recently expanded to "3+5+X," as LMC states have broadened cooperation areas even further to include the digital economy, environmental protection, customs and youth (Xinhua 2019). At the very least, the launch of the LMC illustrates China's willingness to discuss its development activity along the Lancang-Mekong River in a multilateral context (Biba 2018). Given the broad scope and a focus on development, "mutual benefit" is an important foundation of the relationship (LMC 2018a, 2018b), allowing for reciprocal exchange across this broad array of cooperation areas. It is also in the context of the Lancang-Mekong River and LMC where an emphasis on reciprocity has been most explicit. In 2016, after a serious drought in the Lancang-Mekong region China was the target of significant criticism, accused in the media of being an "upstream water controller" (Chellaney 2016). In response, an article, written by Chinese scholars and practitioners, was posted on the website of the Chinese Embassy in Bangkok, aiming to debunk those claims.[4]

Table 2.4 A selection of water governance documents related to the Lancang-Mekong Cooperation (LMC) Mechanism

Signatory	*Document*
Cambodia, China, Laos, Thailand, Myanmar, Vietnam	2016 Sanya Declaration 2018 Phnom Penh Declaration 2018 Five Year Action Plan on LMC (2018–2022) 2018 Kunming Initiative
LMC-MRC	2019 Memorandum of Understanding between the LMC Water Resources Cooperation Center and MRC

Note

* For a complete, and regularly updated timeline of the Lancang-Mekong Cooperation Mechanism, including related documents, see Devlaeminck 2020.

In doing so, it explicitly mentioned the need for a "universal understanding of reciprocity rights and responsibilities" so as to build trust on the Lancang-Mekong, while also indicating that just like all riparians, China, an upstream state, has "reciprocal rights and responsibilities" (Tian & Liu 2016).

Conclusion

Even though China has often had a difficult relationship with the international legal system, it has "slowly grown on China" as it has become more familiar with international law and the benefits it can bring (Saul 2013: 210). Although its relationship with international law continues to evolve, this step-by-step acceptance and participation in international law has been founded upon the notion of reciprocity, apparent throughout the history of its international engagement from the tribute system to modern-day. China's history with international law has established a strong emphasis on state sovereignty, evident through the Five Principles of Peaceful Coexistence, and their placing of mutual respect for territorial integrity and sovereignty front and centre. China's transboundary waters follow a similar approach, emphasizing the Five Principles and sovereignty as explored in this chapter through the preamble and scope of various agreements and, the general scope of cooperation in instances where these agreements are few. China's transboundary waters, divided here between the Northeast, Northwest and Southwest, and the agreements that govern them include explicit and implicit mention of reciprocity and the Five Principles. What differs between these regions, however, is the scope of these agreements. China's agreements are largely bilateral, with the scope of bilateral agreements in the Northwest and Northeast, where legal cooperation is most developed, covering transboundary waters specifically. Multilateral agreements in the region, specifically the Tumen Initiative, have a broad scope covering a variety of issues. In the Southwest, legal cooperation is growing, but it differs significantly from other regions.

In the Southwest, where China has the most riparians and where it has faced criticism due to its upstream hydropower development, the preamble of various agreements does not explicitly mention the Five Principles and reciprocity. These agreements are also narrow in scope, mostly related to information sharing. The exception to this is the LMC and related documents, which is founded upon reciprocal principles. It also has a broad scope, going well beyond water resources. Although the preamble and scope of China's transboundary water agreements identify that China's agreements will be based upon reciprocity and state sovereignty, its unclear what this means in terms of its legal practice. As will be discussed in the following chapters, China's practice and emphasis on the Five Principles and a reciprocal approach aligns with the norms of the global water conventions, including the notion of limited territorial sovereignty, as well as the substantive and procedural rules.

Notes

1 It should be noted that the Covid-19 pandemic has provided many challenges for China and its relations with other states and the international legal system. This experience is certain to shape China's perception and practice of international law, but its long term impact remains unclear.
2 Balance and reciprocity are not necessary for a treaty to be considered as legally valid. As Peters points out, VCLT, Article 2 does not include a reciprocal balance in the definition of a treaty and treaties without a reciprocal balance, such as those governing community interests, are becoming increasingly prevalent (Peters 2007; VCLT 1969: art. 2(1)).
3 The Heilong-Amur forms the border between Russia and China. That being said, with its many tributaries shared between China and Russia it has been described as a "classic example of transboundary river network" (Simonov & Egidarev 2017: 775). While the Heilong-Amur river itself originates in China (forming at the confluence of the Shilka and Argun rivers), two upstream tributaries (the Onon and Kerulen/Kherlen) originate in Mongolia.
4 Admittedly this is not a government-issued document, but its posting to the Embassy website indicates, at the very least, a level of endorsement of its content.

References

Basist, A., & Williams, C. (2020). Monitoring the Quantity of Water Flowing Through the Upper Mekong Basin Under Natural (Unimpeded) Conditions. Eyes on Earth. Retrieved from https://558353b6-da87-4596-a181-b1f20782dd18.filesusr.com/ugd/bae95b_0e0f87104dc8482b99ec91601d853122.pdf?index=true

Bernauer, T., Dong, L., McGrath, L. F., Shaymerdenova, I. & Zhang, H. (2016). Unilateral or Reciprocal Climate Policy? Experimental Evidence from China. *Politics and Governance*, *4*(3), 152–71.

Biba, S. (2018). China's "Old" and "New" Mekong River Politics: The Lancang-Mekong Cooperation From a Comparative Benefit Sharing Perspective. *Water International*, *43*(5), 622–41.

Bodansky, D. (2010). *The Art and Craft of International Environmental Law*. Cambridge/London: Harvard University Press.

Brunée, J. (1989). "Common Interest" – Echoes from an Empty Shell? Some Thoughts on Common Interest and International Environmental Law. *ZaoRV*, *49*(3–4), 791–808.

Burnay, M. (2018). *Chinese Perspectives on the International Rule of Law: Law and Politics in the One-Party State.* Cheltenham/Northampton: Edward Elgar.

Chan, P. C. W. (2015). *China, State Sovereignty and International Legal Order.* Leiden/Boston: Brill-Nijhoff.

Chellaney, B. (2016). China's Water Hegemony in Asia. *The Washington Times* – April 26. Retrieved from www.washingtontimes.com/news/2016/apr/26/brahma-chellaney-chinas-water-hegemony-in-asia/

Chen, A. (2013). *The Voice from China: An Chen on International Economic Law.* Berlin/Heidelberg: Springer.

Chen, H., Rieu-Clarke, A. & Wouters, P. (2013). Exploring China's Transboundary Water Treaty Practice Through the Prism of the UN Watercourses Convention. *Water International*, *38*(2), 217–30.

Chen, X.-P. & Chen, C. C. (2004). On the Intricacies of the Chinese Guanxi: A Process Model of Guanxi Development. *Asia Pacific Journal of Management*, *21*, 305–24.

Canada–China (2012). Agreement Between the Government of Canada and the Government of the People's Republic of China for the Promotion and Reciprocal Protection of Investments (signed December 5, 2012).

China–India (1954). Agreement between the Republic of India and the People's Republic of China on Trade and Intercourse between the Tibet Region of China and India (signed April 29, 1954).

China–India (2003). Declaration on Principles for Relations and Comprehensive Cooperation (signed June 23, 2003).

China–Italy (1985). Agreement between the Government of the People's Republic of China and the Government of Italy Concerning the Encouragement and Reciprocal Protection of Investments (signed January 28, 1985).

China–Kazakhstan (2001). Agreement on Cooperation in the Use and Protection of Transboundary Rivers (signed February 22, 2001).

China–Mongolia (1962). Border Treaty (signed December 26, 1962).

China–Mongolia (1994). Agreement on the Protection and Utilization of Transboundary Waters (signed April 29, 1993).

China–USA (1972). Joint Communiqué of the People's Republic of China and the United States of America (Shanghai Communiqué) (February 28).

China–USA (2014). Joint Announcement on Climate Change. (Beijing) *The White House Office of the Press Secretary* – November 11. Retrieved from https://obamawhitehouse.archives.gov/the-press-office/2014/11/11/us-china-joint-announcement-climate-change

China–USA (2015). Joint Presidential Statement on Climate Change. (Washington, DC) *The White House Office of the Press Secretary* – September 25. Retrieved from https://obamawhitehouse.archives.gov/the-press-office/2015/09/25/us-china-joint-presidential-statement-climate-change

China–USA. (2016). Joint Presidential Statement on Climate Change. (Washington, DC) *The White House Office of the Press Secretary* – March 31. Retrieved from https://obamawhitehouse.archives.gov/the-press-office/2016/03/31/us-china-joint-presidential-statement-climate-change

Cohen, J. A. (1973). China and Intervention: Theory and Practice. *University of Pennsylvania Law Review, 121*(3), 471–505.

Cohen, J. A. (2019). Law and Power in China's International Relations. *New York University Journal of International Law and Politics, 52*(1), 123–65.

Csikszentmihalyi, M. A. (2008). The Golden Rule in Confucianism. In J. Neusner & B. Chilton (Eds.), *The Golden Rule: The Ethics of Reciprocity in World Religions* (pp. 157–69). New York: Continuum International Publishing Group.

deLisle, J. (2000). China's Approach to International Law: A Historical Perspective. *Proceedings of the Annual Meeting (American Society of International Law), 94*, 267–75.

Devlaeminck, D. J., Wouters, P. & Yang, L. (2020). List of China's Transboundary Water Agreements and Related Documents. *Academia.edu*. Retrieved from https://davidjdevlaeminck.com/research-resources/

Devlaeminck, D. J. (2020). Timeline of the Lancang-Mekong Cooperation (LMC) Mechanism. *Academia.edu*. Retrieved from https://chongqing.academia.edu/DavidDevlaeminck

Dimitrov, R. S. (2010). Inside UN Climate Change Negotiations: The Copenhagen Conference. *Review of Policy Research, 27*(6), 795–821.

Edwards, R. (1987). Imperial China's Border Control Law. *Journal of Chinese Law, 1*, 33–62.

Eyler, B. & Weatherby, C. (2020). Mekong Mainstream Dams as of January 2020. *Stimson Center* – April 2. Retrieved from www.stimson.org/2020/mekong-mainstream-dams-as-of-january-2020/

Falkner, R. (2016). The Paris Agreement and the New Logic of International Climate Politics. *International Affairs, 92*(5), 1107–25.

Fard, S. N. (2016). *Reciprocity in International Law: Its Impact and Function*. Abingdon/New York: Routledge.

Feng, Y., He, D. & Wang, W. (2015). Identifying China's Transboundary Water Risks and Vulnerabilities – A Multidisciplinary Analysis Using Hydrological Data and Legal/Institutional Settings *Water International, 40*(2), 328–41.

Gabbatiss, J. (2019). China's Emissions Could Peak 10 Years Earlier than Paris Climate Pledge. *Carbon Brief* – July 29. Retrieved from www.carbonbrief.org/chinas-emissions-could-peak-10-years-earlier-than-paris-climate-pledge

Gupta, J. (2018). China Resumes Sharing Brahmaputra Water Flow Data with India. *thethirdpole.net* – May 17. Retrieved from www.thethirdpole.net/en/2018/05/17/china-resumes-sharing-brahmaputra-water-flow-data-with-india/

He, D., Wu, R., Feng, Y., Li, Y., Ding, C., Wang, W. & Yu, D. W. (2014). China's Transboundary Waters: New Paradigms for Water and Ecological Security Through Applied Ecology. *The Journal of Applied Ecology, 51*(5), 1159–68.

Ho, S. (2014). River Politics: China's policies in the Mekong and the Brahmaputra in comparative perspective. *Journal of Contemporary China, 23*(85), 1–20.

Ho, S., Qian, N. & Yan, Y. (2019). The Role of Ideas in the China-India Water Dispute. *The Chinese Journal of International Politics, 12*(2), 263–94.

Hu, Y. (2020). River Dams in China Helped Alleviate Drought along Lancang-Mekong, Research Finds. *Global Times* – July 15. Retrieved from www.globaltimes.cn/content/1194654.shtml

Jia, G. (2019). New China and International Law: Practice and Contribution in 70 Years. *Chinese Journal of International Law, 18*(4), 727–50.

Kallio, M., & Fallon, A. (2020). Are China's Dams on the Mekong Causing Downstream Drought? The Importance of Scientific Debate. *Center for Social Development Studies* – April 28. Retrieved from www.csds-chula.org/publications/2020/4/28/critical-nature-are-chinas-dams-on-the-mekong-causing-downstream-drought-the-importance-of-scientific-debate

Keohane, R. O. & Victor, D. G. (2016). Cooperation and Discord in Global Climate Policy. *Nature Climate Change*, *6*, 570–5.

Ketelsen, T., Räsänen, T. A., & Sawdon, J. (2020, 13 May). Did China Turn Off the Lower Mekong? Why Data Matters for Cooperation. *Southeast Asia Globe*. Retrieved from https://southeastasiaglobe.com/china-mekong-river-flow/

Klabbers, J. (2018). Treaties and Their Preambles. In M. Bowman & D. Kritsiotis (Eds.), *Conceptual and Contextual Perspectives on Modern Law of Treaties* (pp. 172–200). Cambridge: Cambridge University Press.

Kyoto Protocol (1997). Kyoto Protocol to the UN Framework on Climate Change (adopted December 11, 1997; entered into force February 16, 2005).

Lam, T. B. (1968). Intervention Versus Tribute in Sino-Vietnamese Relations, 1788–1790. In J. K. Fairbank (Ed.), *The Chinese World Order* (pp. 165–79). Cambridge/London: Harvard University Press.

Lee, S., Hong, I. & Chung, J. (2019). Transboundary Water Cooperation in the Tumen River Basin: A Focus on the Greater Tumen Initiative. *Asia-Pacific Research* , *26*(4), 22–54.

Leggett, J. A., Logan, J. & Mackey, A. (2008). *China's Greenhouse Gas Emissions and Mitigation Policies*. Congressional Research Service. Retrieved from https://fas.org/sgp/crs/row/R41919.pdf

LMC (2016). Sanya Declaration of the First Lancang-Mekong Cooperation (LMC) Leaders' Meeting (adopted March 23, 2016).

LMC (2018a). Five-Year Plan of Action on Lancang-Mekong Cooperation (2018–2022). *China Daily* – January 11. Retrieved from www.chinadaily.com.cn/a/201801/11/WS5a56cd04a3102e5b17374295.html

LMC (2018b). Phnom Penh Declaration of the Second Lancang-Mekong Cooperation (LMC) Leaders' Meeting (adopted January 10, 2018).

Matsushita, M., Schoenbaum, T. J., Mavroidis, P. C. & Hahn, M. (2017). *The World Trade Organization: Law, Practice and Policy* (Vol. 3). Oxford: Oxford University Press.

Mbengue, M. M. (2006). Preamble. In R. Wolfrum (Ed.), *Max Planck Encyclopedias of International Law*, Oxford: Oxford University Press.

McNair, L. (1986). *The Law of Treaties*. Cambridge/London: Cambridge University Press.

MRC (2002). China Signs Data-Sharing Agreement. *Mekong River Commission*. Retrieved from www.mrcmekong.org/assets/Publications/Mekong-News/issue20022AprJun.pdf

MRC (2008). Agreement on Provision of Hydrological Information Renewed by China and MRC. *Mekong River Commission* – 29 August. Retrieved from www.mrcmekong.org/news-and-events/news/agreement-on-provision-of-hydrological-information-renewed-by-china-and-mrc/

MRC (2013). Mekong River Commission and China Boost Water Data Exchange. *Mekong River Commission*- 30 August. Retrieved from www.mrcmekong.org/news-and-events/news/mekong-river-commission-and-china-boost-water-data-exchange/

MRC (2017). The Effects of Chinese Dams on Water Flows in the Lower Mekong Basin. *Mekong River Commission* – June 6. Retrieved from www.mrcmekong.org/news-and-events/news/the-effects-of-chinese-dams-on-water-flows-in-the-lower-mekong-basin/

MRC (2019). State of the Basin Report 2018. Retrieved from www.mrcmekong.org/assets/Publications/SOBR-v8_Final-for-web.pdf

MRC (2020). *Understanding the Mekong River's Hydrological Conditions: A brief commentary note on the "Monitoring the Quantity of Water Flowing Through the Upper Mekong Basin Under Natural (Unimpeded) Conditions" study by Alan Basist and Claude Williams.* Retrieved from www.mrcmekong.org/assets/Publications/Understanding-Mekong-River-hydrological-conditions_2020.pdf

Orakhelashvili, A. (2019). *Akehurst's Modern Introduction to International Law.* Abingdon/New York: Routledge.

Pan, J. (2011). Chinese Philosophy and International Law. *Asian Journal of International Law, 1*, 223–48.

Panda, A. (2017). The Political Geography of the India-China Crisis at Doklam. *The Diplomat* – 13 July. Retrieved from https://thediplomat.com/2017/07/the-political-geography-of-the-india-china-crisis-at-doklam/

Pauwelyn, J. (2003). *Conflict of Norms in Public International Law: How WTO Law Relates to Other Rules of International Law.* Cambridge: Cambridge University Press.

Pennetier, M. (2019). China, France Reaffirm Support of Paris Climate Agreement, Call it "Irreversible." *Reuters* – November 5. Retrieved from www.reuters.com/article/us-china-france-paris-agreement/china-france-reaffirm-support-of-paris-climate-agreement-call-it-irreversible-idUSKBN1XG0QJ

Peters, A. (2007). Treaties, Unequal. In *Max Planck Encylopedia of Public International Law.* Oxford University Press.

Petersmann, E. U. (2012). *International Economic Law in the 21st Century: Constitutional Pluralism and Multilevel Governance of Interdependent Public Goods.* Oxford/Portland: Hart Publishing.

PRC (1982). Constitution of the People's Republic of China (adopted December 4, 1982).

Räsänen, T. A., Someth, P., Lauri, H., Koponen, J., Sarkkula, J. & Kummu, M. (2017). Observed River Discharge Changes due to Hydropower Operations in the Upper Mekong Basin. *Journal of Hydrology, 545*, 28–41.

Saul, B. (2013). China, Natural Resources, Sovereignty and International Law. *Asian Studies Review, 37*(2), 196–214.

Saul, B. (2019). *International Law in the Asia Pacific: A Marriage of Convenience.* Chatham House. Retrieved from www.chathamhouse.org/sites/default/files/CHHJ7378-International-Law-Research-Paper-INT-191031-WEB.pdf

Schwarz, B., Trommsdorff, G., Zheng, G. & Shi, S. (2010). Reciprocity in Intergenerational Support: A Comparison of Chinese and German Adult Daughters. *Journal of Family Issues, 31*(2), 234–56.

Shen, W. & Xie, L. (2019). Can China Lead in Multilateral Environmental Negotiations? Internal Politics, Self-Depiction and China's Contribution in Climate Change Regime and Mekong Governance. *Eurasian Geography and Economics, 59*(5–6), 708–32.

Simma, B. (2008). Reciprocity. In R. Wolfrum (Ed.), *Max Planck Encyclopedias of International Law*. Oxford: Oxford University Press.

Simonov, E. & Egidarev, E. (2017). Intergovernmental Cooperation on the Amur River Basin Management in the Twenty-First Century. *International Journal of Water Resources Development, 34*(5), 771–91.

Stone, C. D. (2004). Common but Differentiated Responsibilities in International Law. *American Journal of International Law, 98*, 276–301.

Stroik, P., Chakraborty, D., Ge, W., Boulter, J. & Jamelske, E. (2019). Effect of Reciprocity on Public Opinion of International Climate Treaties: Experimental Evidence from the US and China. *Climate Policy, 19*(8), 959–73.

Su, Y. (2014). Contemporary Legal Analysis of China's Transboundary Water Regimes: International Law in Practice. *Water International, 39*(5), 705–24.

Tian, F. & Liu, H. (2016). "China's Water Hegemony in Asia" or "Shared Rivers, Shared Futures": Which? *Embassy of the People's Republic of China in the Kingdom of Thailand* – July 27. Retrieved from http://th.china-embassy.org/eng/ztbd/t1384905.htm

Tumen (China-DPRK-Mongolia-ROK-Russia) (1994). Memorandum of Understanding on Environmental Principles Governing the Tumen River Economic Development Area and Northeast Asia (adopted January 1, 1994).

Tvinnereim, E., Chapelle, E. L. & Borick, C. (2016). Is Support for International Climate Action Conditional on Perceptions of Reciprocity? Evidence from Survey Experiments in Canada, The US, Norway and Sweden. *COSMOS, 12*(1), 43–55.

UNCTAD (2020). China. *Investment Policy Hub*. Retrieved from https://investmentpolicy.unctad.org/international-investment-agreements/countries/42/china

UNFCCC (1992). United Nations Framework Convention on Climate Change (adopted May 9, 1992; entered into force March 21, 1994).

UN Charter (1945). Charter of the United Nations (adopted June 26, 1945; entered into force October 24, 1945).

UNGA (1970). Declaration on Principles of International Law concerning Friendly Relations and Co-operation among States in accordance with the Charter of the United Nations, Res. 2625 XXV (October 24, 1970). Retrieved from www.un.org/ga/search/view_doc.asp?symbol=A/RES/2625(XXV)

UNGA (1997). 99th Plenary Meeting, Fifty-First Session, United Nations General Assembly, A/51/PV.99 (January 1, 1997). Retrieved from https://documents-dds-ny.un.org/doc/UNDOC/GEN/N97/855/72/pdf/N9785572.pdf?OpenElement

UNTC (2020). Multilateral Treaties Deposited with the Secretary-General – China. United Nations Treaty Collection. Retrieved from https://treaties.un.org/Pages/TreatyParticipantSearch.aspx?clang=_en

Vattel, E. D. (2008). *The Law of Nations*. Indianapolis: Liberty Fund.

VCLT (1969). Vienna Convention on the Law of Treaties (adopted May 23, 1969; entered into force January 27, 1980).

Wang, T. (1990). International Law in China: Historical and Contemporary Perspectives. *Recueil de Cours, 221*, 199–369.

Water Convention (1992). Convention on the Protection and Use of Transboundary Watercourses and International Lakes (adopted on March 17, 1992; entered into force October 6, 1996).

Watercourses Convention (1997). United Nations Convention on the Law of Non-Navigational Uses of International Watercourses (adopted on May 21, 1997; entered into force August 17, 2014).

Watts, S. (2009). Reciprocity and the Law of War. *Harvard International Law Journal, 50*(2), 365–434.

Westwood, R., Chan, A. & Linstead, S. (2004). Theorizing Chinese Employment Relations Comparatively: Exchange, Reciprocity and the Moral Economy. *Asia Pacific Journal of Management, 21*, 365–89.

Wouters, P. (2013). *International Law – Facilitating Transboundary Water Cooperation.* Global Water Partnership. Retrieved from www.gwp.org/globalassets/global/toolbox/publications/background-papers/17-international-law--facilitating-transboundary-water-cooperation-2013-english.pdf

Wouters, P. & Chen, H. (2013). China's "Soft-Path" to Transboundary Water Cooperation Examined in the Light of Two UN Global Water Conventions – Exploring the "Chinese Way." *Journal of Water Law, 22*(6), 229–47.

WTO (2001a). Meeting of the Working Party on the Accession of China – Statement by H.E. Vice Minister LONG Yongtu, Head of the Chinese Delegation, at the eighteenth session of the Working Party on China. *WTO News* – September 17. Retrieved from www.wto.org/english/news_e/news01_e/wpchina_longstat_17sept01_e.htm

WTO (2001b). Meeting of the Working Party on the Accession of China – Statement by H.E. Vice Minister LONG Yongtu, Head of the Chinese Delegation, at the sixteenth session of the Working Party on China. *WTO News* – July 4. Retrieved from www.wto.org/english/news_e/news01_e/china_longstat_jul01_e.htm

Wu, X. (2011). No Longer Outside, Not Yet Equal: Rethinking China's Membership in the World Trade Organization. *Chinese Journal of International Law, 10*(2), 227–70.

Xi, J. (2014). Carry forward the Five Principles of Peaceful Coexistence to build a better world through win–win cooperation. *People's Daily*. Retrieved from http://en.people.cn/n/2014/0710/c90883-8753393.html

Xi, J. (2015a). Carry Forward the Bandung Spirit for Win-Win Cooperation: Remarks by Chinese President Xi Jinping *Ministry of Foreign Affairs of the People's Republic of China*. Retrieved from www.fmprc.gov.cn/mfa_eng/wjdt_665385/zyjh_665391/t1259844.shtml

Xi, J. (2015b). Towards a Community of Common Destiny and a New Future for Asia, Keynote Speech, Boao Forum for Asia Annual Conference. Retrieved from http://news.xinhuanet.com/english/2015-03/29/c_134106145.htm

Xie, L. & Jia, S. (2018). *China's International Transboundary Rivers: Politics, Security and Diplomacy of Shared Water Resources*. Abingdon/New York: Routledge.

Xinhua. (2019). Training program launched to bolster Lancang-Mekong Cooperation. *China Daily* – May 7. Retrieved from www.chinadaily.com.cn/a/201905/07/WS5cd13670a3104842260ba503.html

Xue, H. (1992). Relativity in International Water Law. *Colorado Journal of International Environmental Law and Policy, 3*, 45–57.

Xue, H. (2005). China's Open Policy and International Law. *Chinese Journal of International Law, 4*(1), 133–9.

Xue, H. (2007). Chinese Observations on International Law. *Chinese Journal of International Law, 6*(1), 83–93.

Xue, H. (2011). Chinese Contemporary Perspectives on International Law: History, Culture and International Law. *Recueil des cours, 355*, 47–220.

Yasuda, Y., Aich, D., Hill, D., Huntjens, P. & Swain, A. (2017). *Transboundary Water Cooperation over the Brahmaputra River: Legal Political Economy Analysis of Current and Future Potential Cooperation*. The Hague Institute for Global Justice. Retrieved from www.siwi.org/publications/transboundary-water-cooperation-brahmaputra-river-legal-political-economy-analysis-current-future-potential-cooperation/

Zhang, Z., Guo, D. & Luo, Y. (2014). Coresidence with Elderly Parents in Contemporary China: The Role of Filial Piety, Reciprocity, Socioeconomic Resources and Parental Needs. *Journal of Cross Cultural Gerentology, 29*, 259–76. doi:10.1007/s10823-014-9239-4

Zhao, S. (2018). A Revisionist Stakeholder: China and the Post-World War II World Order. *Journal of Contemporary China, 27*(113), 643–58.

Zhao, Y. (2017). China has to halt river data sharing as India infringes on sovereignty: expert. *Global Times* – August 20. Retrieved from www.globaltimes.cn/content/1062249.shtml

3 Sovereignty claims in the law of international watercourses

In late 2015, the international community came together to adopt the 2030 Transforming our World document, thus adopting the 2030 Sustainable Development Agenda. This document, referring to itself as a "charter for people and planet in the twenty-first century," contains 17 goals, complemented by 169 targets that the global community wishes to achieve by 2030. Sustainable Development Goal (SDG) 6, directly related to water, aims to "ensure availability and sustainable management of water and sanitation for all" (UNGA 2015). SDG 6.5 specifically aims to implement Integrated Water Resources Management across all levels, including transboundary waters. China, who views the SDGs as a "list of deliverables that carries with it [China's] solemn commitment" (Xi 2015c), has pledged to "enhance the role of comprehensive river basin management in water governance" (MFA 2016a). Given the number of transboundary waters, this commitment will certainly require increased cooperation and collaboration with neighbouring countries. Implementing this goal, however, becomes ever more challenging as climate change affects the hydrologic stationarity of the globe, which will "change a vast array of visible and invisible parameters that define the very foundation of the world as we know it" (UNU-INWEH 2016). As such, it is unclear whether water will be where we need it, when we need it in the future. As China and the world become ever more interconnected, global problems require global solutions, placing pressure on the foundational notions of international law, including sovereignty which is certainly no longer absolute (Crawford 2015). International law is witnessing a series of changes as two of its layers, one deeply rooted in state sovereignty and the other building on community interests, come together (Klein 2011). The law of international watercourses, which tackles some of these complex interconnected challenges, is also witnessing these changes as it incorporates aspects of environmental, human and economic concerns, and shifts away from notions of absolute state sovereignty to incorporate more communal theories of management of shared resources.

Regardless of the changes in the international legal system, the "2030 Transforming our World" agenda reminds us that sovereignty is still foundational to the global legal and political regime. While devoting itself to win–win cooperation and a people-centred approach in the achievement of the SDGs, the document reaffirms sovereignty's role at the heart of the international system, stating that "every state has, and shall freely exercise, full permanent sovereignty over all its wealth, natural resources and economic activity" (UNGA 2015: para. 18). Although China is admittedly a strong supporter of sovereignty, there is little evidence that it supports an absolute form of sovereignty, and thus far China has not made a claim of absolute territorial sovereignty concerning its transboundary waters. In a legal system firmly grounded on the sovereign equality of states, according to Article 2 of the UN Charter, reciprocity will play a pivotal role. As both an "underlying condition of cooperation" (Leb 2013: 29) and as a legal principle, reciprocity works to uphold a level playing field. As a legal principle, it does so by ensuring that states who make claims must accept that others are also able to do so and benefit accordingly. As such, it is one reason why states would limit their claims, ensuring they are reasonable, thereby assisting with the development of customary international law.

Given this background in the international legal system, this chapter aims to survey the development of the law of international watercourses through the lens of one of the factors of its development, reciprocity. In order to do so it will first establish the development of international law as a reciprocal process. It will then turn to apply this to the development of the law of international watercourses through the four primary sovereignty claims, including previous claims of absolute territorial sovereignty and absolute territorial integrity, which have ultimately been set aside to recognize the notion of limited territorial sovereignty. The debate surrounding these notions and tension between these concepts of sovereignty is relevant to China's state practice, as China is often perceived to practice some form of absolute territorial sovereignty. An analysis of this reciprocal process can shed light on the true nature of limited territorial sovereignty. As such the chapter will turn to discuss China's transboundary treaty practice in light of the outlined reciprocal process which results in the notion of limited territorial sovereignty, ultimately claiming that China's state practice is a clear example of limited territorial sovereignty. The chapter will then discuss the fourth, emerging claim of the community of interests so as to explore the role that reciprocity has played within its development, followed by a brief discussion of this notion in China's treaty practice through the concept of the "community of common destiny."

The development of international law as a process of reciprocation

Members of communities often have norms and beliefs in common, and such beliefs are an important factor that helps to establish bonds between community members. Such shared norms and beliefs influence the operation of actions and relations between agents within communities (Fard 2016). As previously discussed, the concept of reciprocity initially emerged as one such belief within social systems, where reciprocity acts as "both a defining feature of social exchange and a source of societal cooperation and solidarity" (Molm 2010: 129). Often discussed as an exchange between agents, reciprocity structures such actions and relations to include both rights and duties, driving people to help those who have helped them, and not to injure those who have helped them (Gouldner 1960). This "mutually gratifying pattern of exchanging goods and services" establishes mutual dependence (Gouldner 1960: 171) and, as such, reciprocal exchange and the expectation of reciprocation assists in the establishment of groups and the emergence of future social exchange.

For states, reciprocity is also a process of exchange through which "potentially antagonistic nations are able to establish cooperation and reach mutually rewarding outcomes" (Patchen 1998: 171). It can also, however, have the opposite effect, and may even lead to "continuing and, possibly escalating, mutual conflict" (Patchen 1998: 171). As a force of cooperation, however, states make concessions in good faith with the expectation that such concessions would be reciprocated. If such concessions are reciprocally returned, they have the potential to lead to further cooperation. If they are not returned or not returned in kind, then good faith is frustrated and cooperation is unlikely to develop. Over time, states' interest in sustained, mutually beneficial relations leads them to reciprocate consistently. Even though the building blocks of cooperation and law are the same (Leb 2014), expectations of reciprocity, as discussed above, should be differentiated from reciprocity as a legal principle. Within highly developed legal systems, reciprocity has been "absorbed and supplanted by specific norms and institutions" (Simma 2008: para. 1). The lower the level of "institutionalization of a legal system, however, the more mechanisms of direct reciprocity" are present (Simma 2008: para. 1). As an "objective aspect of a given legal relationship" (Simma 2008: para. 2) which works to ensure fairness, the principle of reciprocity is a legal consequence of the equality of states (Byers 2004), ensuring that "conduct by one party is in one way or another juridically dependent upon that of the other party" (Paulus 2011: 117). As such, expectations of reciprocity and reciprocity as a legal principle play a strong role within the limitation of state claims, contributing to the establishment of consistent and uniform state practice and, ultimately, customary law.

Given that water is a resource which is absolutely fundamental to both the function of states and the livelihoods of citizens, and that it is often transboundary in nature, cooperation is required so that everyone can meet their needs. With many transboundary basins not covered by common management frameworks (Adeel et al. 2015), customary law will play a particularly important role. Customary law is a unique source of law, as it is not created by decision-makers but by the overall practice of states (Fard 2016). As such, it recognizes the need for consent as well as the dual nature of states as both creators and subjects of international law. The establishment of customary law relies on two conditions: rules of a norm creating character must have substantial 1) state practice and 2) *opinio juris*. State practice must be widespread and uniform, pertaining especially to specifically affected states. It cannot be clumped in various regions, and practice by those particularly affected by the norm in question is of particular importance (Crawford 2012). Article 38c of the Statute of the International Court of Justice (ICJ) indicates that customary law must be "accepted as law," thus introducing the requirement of *opinio juris*. This entails that states must believe that they are legally obligated to carry out such practice, ultimately consenting to it. Through acceptance or rejection, states consent or show their belief that the practice is accepted as law. Such consent is based on reciprocity, as states are unlikely to consent to a rule that is against their reciprocal interests (Fard 2016). Whether or not *opinio juris* is required, however, is a matter of some debate as some argue that it is circular or that the ICJ has paid scant attention to proving its existence in past cases. There are, however, some cases in which the ICJ has indicated its necessity, and it is of incredible importance in lending legitimacy to customary law (Fard 2016; ICJ 1986).

Prior to increasing levels of development there was often enough water within shared basins such that the use of one state would not affect the uses or interests of their riparian neighbours. As states developed so too did their water usage, and as such so too did their impact on upstream or downstream riparians. At the beginning of the 19th century when water uses began to develop and states' water interests began to conflict, states had to rely upon general principles as the body of law surrounding transboundary waters was relatively underdeveloped (McCaffrey 1996). The formation of customary law can be described as a process of cooperation or conflict, where either customary law forms as a result of overall agreement or does not form owing to disagreement. In this process, reciprocity and expectations of reciprocity go hand-in-hand to "moderate the claims put forward by a state initiating the law-making process," and "facilitate the acceptance of such claims" from states who may wish to make similar claims in the future (Simma 2008: para. 3).

Within international law, "a state basing a claim on a particular norm of international law must accept that rule as also binding upon itself" (Simma 2008: para. 2), exemplified in both the Vienna Convention on the Law of Treaties (VCLT) and the Statute of the ICJ. The VCLT, which has an overall tone of reciprocity, stipulates that all states have the right to enter into treaties, with both rights and obligations that are equally binding on all parties (VCLT 1969: art. 6). The jurisdiction of the ICJ is also based on this understanding of reciprocity, as only parties who reciprocate their consent to the ICJ can bring cases before the Court (ICJ 1945: art. 36). In other words, "any state claiming a right under that law has to accord all other states the same right" (Byers 2004: 89). As such, reciprocity moderates the claims that states make in three ways: First, the reciprocity of claims ensures that states will only claim things that they wish to see generalized. Second, if states see no potential benefit in the new claim then they may not support it, and may even oppose it by seeking to establish alternative claims. Third, reciprocity limits the benefits of being a persistent objector since other states can also claim such an objection (Byers 2004).

Reciprocation and the development of limited territorial sovereignty

In instances of state conflict concerning their shared water resources, it has often been the case that upstream states make claims of absolute territorial sovereignty, claiming that the water within their territory is their own and that they can do with it as they please. Downstream states, however, often make claims of absolute territorial integrity, claiming that the upstream state cannot take any action that would affect flows to the downstream state. When analysed through the lens of reciprocity, however, neither claim is tenable and may even harm the long-term interests of both upstream and downstream states. The interconnectivity of water, however, brings states together in the name of cooperation. This section aims to trace the development of the law of international watercourses through the sovereignty claims that have come to define it. In order to do so, it will analyse the claims of absolute territorial sovereignty in the *Rio Grande Dispute* between the United States of America (USA) and Mexico, and absolute territorial integrity in the *Trail Smelter Case* between Canada and the USA. When analysed through a lens of reciprocity, however, neither claim is acceptable and the law of international watercourses has ultimately settled on a claim in the middle as custom, namely limited territorial sovereignty.

Absolute territorial sovereignty and absolute territorial integrity

The most notable example of absolute territorial sovereignty is the Harmon Doctrine elicited by Judge Judson Harmon, an American Attorney General in the late 19th century. A dispute arose between Mexico and the USA owing to a diversion of the waters of the Rio Grande by farmers and ranchers in Colorado and New Mexico when the water levels near Ciudad Juarez along the Mexico–USA border were severely reduced (McCaffrey 2019). The Mexican minister at Washington, in a letter to the Secretary of State outlining the urgency of the situation, claimed that the low water levels would threaten the existence of various communities south of the border. The USA government claimed that it was uncertain if their actions were the cause, and ultimately referred the situation to the Attorney General, Judson Harmon. Tasked with determining whether Mexico's claims were valid within the general body of international law, Judge Harmon, citing the principle of sovereignty, claimed that "all exceptions [...] to the full and complete power of a nation within its own territories must be traced up to the consent of the nation itself" (McCaffrey 2019: 102). Thus, any right to waters within American territory by Mexico were inconsistent with the principle of sovereignty. Judge Harmon concluded that at the time the rules and principles of international law "impose no liability or obligation upon the United States" and that the principle of sovereignty provides states with "full and complete power over a nation within its territory" (McCaffrey 2019: 102).

Surprisingly, the most notable example of a claim of absolute territorial integrity is also from the USA. In 1925 when the Trail Smelter in British Columbia, Canada, expanded production and increased the height of its smoke stacks, Washington state experienced increased crop scorching and forest loss owing to pollution drifting downwind. What started as a minor dispute quickly escalated and the case was referred to the International Joint Commission (IJC) through an Arbitral Commission (Wirth 1996). In the dispute, the USA State Department made claims of absolute territorial integrity when its legal adviser claimed that the principle of sovereignty ensures that "a sovereign state is supreme within its own territorial domain and that it and its nationals are entitled to use and enjoy their territory and property without interference from an outside source" (McCaffrey 2019: 117). Given the reciprocal nature of claims within international law, states must be willing to accept the generalization of their claims. As such, a state that makes a claim must accept that other states can also make the same claims and benefit accordingly. In so doing, reciprocity ensures that states will only claim that which they wish to see generalized (Byers 2004). Thus, if a state bases its claim on the principle of sovereignty and claims that this principle entails absolute territorial sovereignty or absolute territorial integrity then it must reciprocate and allow others to do so as well. Given the nature of water resources and the requirement of generalization within international law, making claims of absolute territorial sovereignty or absolute territorial integrity is untenable. At their core, such extreme sovereignty claims hinder the ability of riparian states to utilize waters within their territories, ignoring the necessity of water utilization and the interconnected nature of transboundary water resources. This harms the balance struck by the formal equality of states. Given that states are often both upstream and downstream, however, acceptance of such extreme claims are often not in a state's interests. In these situations, such a claim can provide benefits in one basin, but hinder the same state in another where they are in a different geographical position, as was the case of the USA in these disputes.

Interestingly, neither of these extreme claims to sovereignty was featured in their resolution. Instead, both cases were resolved while recognizing the rights of their riparian neighbours. In spite of Judge Harmon's opinion that the USA had no legal obligations under international law, the USA and Mexico proceeded with joint fact-finding, which recommended that a treaty be signed between the two countries that would distribute the waters equally through the construction of an American funded dam at El Paso. After which, Mexico would abandon any claims of indemnity for previous unlawful uses of the shared water resources (McCaffrey 1996). In spite of the controversy surrounding dam construction on the Rio Grande,[1] a dam was constructed on the river at Engle, New Mexico. The dispute was finally put to rest with the signing of the 1906 Convention between the United States and Mexico: Equitable Distribution of the Waters of the Rio Grande, which cites the "equitable distribution of the waters of the Rio Grande" as its intended purpose (Mexico–USA 1906).

In this dispute, American actors walked a fine line between recognition of the rights of Mexico and maintaining their claim of absolute territorial sovereignty. Even though the treaty aims to distribute waters in an equitable and reasonable manner between both riparians, it maintains the American legal position of absolute territorial sovereignty by limiting its scope to the "portion of the Rio Grande which forms the international boundary," and by stating that the USA does not accept "any legal basis for claims heretofore asserted or which may be hereafter asserted by reason of any losses incurred by the owners of land in Mexico due or alleged to be due to the diversion" of the river. Furthermore, the USA did not "in any way concede the establishment of any general principle or precedent by the concluding of this treaty" (Mexico–USA 1906: art. 5). Thus, the USA recognized the rights of Mexico to the utilization of its waters by aiming towards "equitable distribution" within the treaty. The treaty itself, however, states that such practice does not support the establishment of a general principle. In spite of USA officials arguing that sovereignty permits absolute control over transboundary resources within a nation's own territory, looking at the entirety of its state practice in this instance illustrates that the USA did not believe it was legally permitted to follow through with such a claim (McCaffrey 1996). Although explicitly stating that these claims do not establish any form of precedent, reciprocity and the generalization of claims may have been a factor that affected its variations in practice. If the USA were to firmly claim absolute territorial sovereignty over the Rio Grande, then it may be at a disadvantage and lead to problems in instances where it is downstream from its neighbours, as was the case in the *Trail Smelter Case.*

In spite of the fact that American practice surrounding the *Rio Grande Dispute* maintained a fine line between recognition of the rights of riparians and claims of absolute territorial sovereignty, the *Trail Smelter Case* was more clearly resolved through recognition of the rights of both riparians to utilize their shared resources. As stated earlier, the case was referred to the IJC and, after fact-finding to determine the extent and seriousness of the damage, it was concluded that "under the principles of international law, as well as the law of the United States, no state has the right to use or permit the use of its territory in such a manner as to cause injury by fumes in or to the territory of another" (IJC 1941). In its decision, the tribunal stated that each party

> [h]as an equal interest that if a nuisance is proved, the indemnity to damaged parties for proven damage shall be just and adequate and each also has an equal interest that unproven or unwarranted claims shall not

> be allowed. For, while the United States' interests may now be claimed to be injured by the operations of a Canadian corporation, it is equally possible that at some time in the future Canadian interests might be claimed to be injured by an American Corporation.
>
> (IJC 1941: 1938–9)

Such "reciprocity of risk" has been cited as one reason why the USA was unwilling to enter into such deliberations (Mickelson 1993: 228), since if Canada was to suspend the operation of the Trail Smelter or owe an indemnity to the US, then it is highly likely that Canada could pursue the USA in court regarding similar issues in the more highly developed eastern portion of the Canada–USA border (Read 1963).[2] Furthermore, if the claims of absolute territorial integrity were upheld, third parties might then be able to claim damages through the precedent such a decision could establish. As such, American officials were treading carefully given that claims on its northern border could also affect its southern border with Mexico, as evidenced by industry surveys indicating concern amongst industries along the southern border (Wirth 1996).

The emergence of limited territorial sovereignty

As stated above, absolute territorial sovereignty and absolute territorial integrity could have devastating impacts for either upstream or downstream riparians. That being said, they are often claimed as advocacy tools and not as reflections of the legal obligations that states believe they have (McCaffrey 2019). As we saw in the *Rio Grande* and *Trail Smelter* disputes, state claims and actions were at times not aligned, and it appears that the USA did not believe that a claim to absolute territorial sovereignty or absolute territorial integrity met its obligations concerning transboundary waters. The resolution of these two cases established a third claim of sovereignty which has been accepted as customary international law, namely that of limited territorial sovereignty. Limited territorial sovereignty recognizes the equal rights of all riparian states to the usage of shared waters, and that riparian states must respect the claims of others on its shared watercourse (McCaffrey 2019). Thus, a state claiming limited territorial sovereignty is more likely willing to generalize such a claim, since this would ensure mutual respect of the rights of both states, independent of their geographical position. State practice has also revolved around the acceptance of this claim, recognized through the adoption of various treaties and subsequent state practice. This is most notable in the principles of equitable and reasonable use as well as the due diligence obligation not to cause significant harm, both of which have also been accepted as custom (see ICJ 1997) and codified most notably in the 1966 Helsinki Rules, the 1997 United Nations Convention on the Law of Non-navigational Uses of International Watercourses (Watercourses Convention) and the 1992 United Nations Economic Commission for Europe (UNECE) Convention on the

Protection and Use of Transboundary Watercourses and International Lakes (Water Convention). The international legal regime which has emerged from this foundation in limited territorial sovereignty will be discussed further in Chapters 4 and 5.

Even though limited territorial sovereignty and the substantive rules that have emerged from it have been accepted as custom, there are a series of rules that are arguably not yet recognized as custom but could be considered to be moving closer towards recognition as such, namely the duty to conduct an environmental impact assessment (EIA) or the duty to suspend. Such procedural cooperative obligations flow from the concept of limited territorial sovereignty, and are often necessary in order to determine what is equitable and reasonable, and to prevent significant harm or determine instances where harm has occurred. Reciprocity may also play a role in their further development and eventual acceptance as customary law. For example, the duty to conduct a transboundary EIA is widely accepted and has been described as an "emerging principle of international law" (McIntyre 2007: 239). Considered as a possible requirement under general international law in relation to projects which may have negative impacts within the *Pulp Mills Case* (ICJ 2010), the duty to conduct an EIA is part of the process of consultation and notification. Even though it may be considered a part of general international law, the duty to conduct an EIA is highly context-dependent, leaving considerable room for states to determine its content. Reciprocity may be one factor which assists states in determining the baseline content of such duties in like situations and thus push towards the crystallization of these laws into custom. Through reciprocity, states will only make claims that they wish to see generalized, and so states will act in their procedural duties in ways they wish their neighbours to act in hopes of reciprocation, possibly stimulating further cooperation. At present there is very little guidance in relation to the content of EIA. Three basic components of a good assessment have been identified, including: 1) an EIA must be undertaken during the planning stage of the project so that the results can be taken into consideration prior to implementation; 2) that without consultation with affected states the proposing state must not proceed with its project; and 3) that the EIA must identify the nature and consequences of the proposed project (McIntyre 2007). Reciprocation between parties will assist in ensuring that states conduct reasonable assessments that they would also find acceptable in the other situations.

China's practice as limited territorial sovereignty

The legal notion of reciprocity will work to limit such claims in states that are both upstream and downstream. Such a requirement of reciprocity, however, may not be enough to limit state claims concerning transboundary waters in some situations. While it can be difficult to categorize states into upstream or downstream given the geographical contours of shared waters, some states are almost entirely upstream or downstream from their riparian neighbours. These states, particularly those that are primarily upstream, may be in a geographical position to make and maintain claims of absolute territorial sovereignty or absolute territorial integrity without negative repercussions. These states may believe that they do not need to generalize such claims, since given their upstream position they are unlikely to feel many, if any, negative impacts in relation to transboundary waters. Such states may even be able to act as a persistent objector, a state who "persistently and consistently objects to a newly emerging norm of customary international law" during the formation of that norm, and who is therefore not bound by that norm (Green 2016: 1). This would, however, require the satisfaction of various criterion, including that its "objection must be clearly expressed, made known to other states and maintained persistently" (ILC 2018: 152).

Authors have claimed that China, as an upstream state, practices some form of absolute territorial sovereignty (for example, Chellaney 2013; Liebman 2005; Menniken 2007) acting in some ways as a persistent objector that challenges the existence of customary legal norms. Although beyond the analysis conducted here, given that China has not previously made a claim of absolute territorial sovereignty it is highly unlike that in the case of China these criteria have been met. Even if upstream states can, due to their geographical position, maintain these claims, reciprocity can act as a powerful reason why states would not do so. First, even though states may be able to maintain such claims, being entirely upstream or downstream is not the only relevant factor states will take into consideration when making these decisions. Reciprocation does not need to occur in the same transaction or the same issue area (Dinar 2008; Keohane 1986) and in interconnected issue areas of common interest such as water, persistent objection will bring few benefits. Thus, if states do not recognize the rights of riparians to the use of their shared waters their neighbours may reciprocate negatively in other areas, potentially establishing a long-term path of negative reciprocation and conflict between them.

Second, such a disregard for the common interests shared with their neighbours may damage a state's reputation and thereby its ability to work together with neighbouring states in the future. Reputation and reciprocity go hand-in-hand, and a state that reciprocates positive behaviour will receive a positive reputation, whereas states that fail to reciprocate positive behaviour or return positive behaviour with negative behaviour will not. A reputation for complying with international law provides states with credibility and a reputation as a good partner, making it easier to enter into future cooperative agreements and receive more favourable concessions from their partners, ultimately making such cooperation more fruitful (Guzman 2008). Thus, states are more likely to reciprocate and generalize claims in order to keep in good standing with their neighbours. While there may be no exchange of actual goods or services between states in these instances, reputation and trust may also act as a form of exchange. Such an exchange may include the exchange of benefits, services or cooperation for positive reputation (Mushkat 2011) and a trusting more fruitful relationship. As there are very few states that would be able to maintain such claims in relation to their transboundary waters, its effect on state practice and *opinio juris* may be minimal.[3] In spite of this, it could be argued that a few powerful states may have more influence on the creation of custom, and may even be able to influence the practice of other states. Such states may be able to absorb the reputational impact while reaping greater benefits. Although this may be hypothetically possible, in the context of transboundary waters there are instances where even powerful states who are primarily upstream or downstream have moved towards cooperation, and, more often than not, conflicting views result in compromise and cooperation instead of conflict, as is the case with China.

China's transboundary water treaty practice: limited territorial sovereignty

It has been perceived that China, as an upstream state, practices some form of absolute territorial sovereignty, acting in some ways as a persistent objector that challenges the existence of customary legal norms. An analysis of its state practice illustrates that this is not the case. Citing China's vote against the Watercourses Convention, its construction of dams on the upper reaches of the Lancang-Mekong River, diversions of the Irtysh River, and non-river related issues such China's claims on the South China Sea,[4] Ho argues that "China cooperates when it is in its interests to do so and when it perceives benefits from cooperation, and not because it observes limited territorial sovereignty" (Ho 2017: 148). There is a growing body of literature, however, which argues that China does indeed practice some form of limited territorial sovereignty (Chen et al. 2013; Han 2017; Su 2014; Wouters & Chen 2013). From a *legal perspective*, becoming a party to a treaty is in itself an act of sovereignty which places limitations on that sovereignty (Wang 1990). In transboundary waters, these treaties ensure that "national interests and actions are prescribed and circumscribed through rules of international law, both substantive and procedural" (Wouters 2014: 73), thus recognizing the importance of national interests while balancing them with those of riparian neighbours.

China's upstream position may permit it to maintain and practice absolute territorial sovereignty; however, analysis of its state practice illustrates that it does not. Concerning the transboundary waters between China and its neighbours, trust is a significant issue. China, however, is striving to create a reputation as a "good neighbour," slowly moving towards recognition of the rights of its riparian neighbours (Wouters 2014: 72). As a signatory to approximately 70 treaties and other documents governing or related to transboundary waters (Devlaeminck et al. 2020), China accepts the principles of equitable and reasonable use, as well as no-significant harm. Such principles are mentioned in many of its treaties, discussed further in Chapter 4; however, they are often underdeveloped within these documents (Wouters & Chen 2013). Thus, from a legal perspective China clearly practices limited territorial sovereignty as it has chosen to limit and contour its actions through a series of treaties and agreements that concern its transboundary waters. As a legal principle, reciprocity ensures that "conduct by one party is in one way or another juridically dependent upon that of the other party" (Paulus 2011: 117). This limits state claims, since any state which makes a claim based upon a particular norm must be ready to give other states that same right (Simma 2008). As such, states are unlikely to make claims they are not willing to see generalized (Byers 2004). States choose, based on their sovereignty, to limit their own practices. Such a compromise is based upon the interdependence of the community of states and recognition that you will be better off recognizing the rights of others, instead of only recognizing their own. States are aware that their claims of absolute territorial sovereignty or absolute territorial integrity could be used against them on their transboundary waters or in other areas of cooperation due to the linkages between water and other issue areas such as energy, agriculture, trade, and more. This reciprocal process of its development is very telling of the nature of limited territorial sovereignty as an approach of enlightened self-interest, not of altruism.

China cooperates on its transboundary waters when it is in its interests to do so, as do many other states. This does not, however, preclude characterizing its practice as limited territorial sovereignty. Through its acceptance of limited territorial sovereignty, evidenced by the limitations it has placed on its sovereignty through its acceptance and participation in a series of legal frameworks, China has participated in a process of reciprocation through which cooperation and trust can grow in a step-by-step approach (Leb 2014). Such an approach has led to higher levels of cooperation, especially in its Northern regions, through which both states can benefit. For example, China–Kazakhstan cooperation has developed due to a strategy of issue-linkage, a non-explicit exchange that often takes place during negotiations, as the two cooperate on various issues ranging from anti-terrorism measures, energy, intelligence, and more (Ho 2017), permitting these states to build trust. This trust-building has resulted in the signing of multiple agreements concerning transboundary waters, most notably the 2001 China–Kazakhstan Agreement on Cooperation in the Use and Protection of Transboundary Rivers. This strategy of issue-linkage, however, is not without its disadvantages, as it could also be used by more powerful states to extract concessions from weaker parties (Ho 2017). While cooperation on its Southwest basins has yet to fully develop, such issue-linkage and reciprocity is one strategy that states could use, and is already taking place through a possible informal benefit-sharing regime with the potential to lead to more formalized cooperation through legal frameworks. China is increasingly dependent on its southern neighbours for energy and as such requires a healthy and stable relationship with them (Lee 2015; Ptak & Hommel 2016).

Such reciprocity and issue-linkage, especially regarding energy production in China's southern neighbours, will arguably lead to further integration and cooperation in their transboundary rivers, potentially through the new

Lancang-Mekong Cooperation (LMC) Mechanism. Although not a party to the 1995 Agreement on the Cooperation for the Sustainable Development of the Mekong River Basin, in November 2015 China hosted the 1st LMC Mechanisms Foreign Minister's Meeting, which officially launched the LMC Mechanism. The LMC Mechanism is not a water-sharing agreement and the legal nature of the related documents is unclear, it may present opportunities for issue-linkage and to ultimately develop into a legal framework if its members wish to do so. Based on consensus, mutual benefit and equality, all parties, including representatives from Thailand, Vietnam, Myanmar, Laos, Cambodia and China, agreed on its future direction and to enhance cooperation concerning priority areas, including water (MFA 2016b). In March 2016 all riparian countries once again came together, resulting in the Sanya Declaration in which riparian states recognize that "our security and development interests are closely inter-connected," and thus the parties devote themselves to increasing cooperation based upon "equality, mutual consultation and coordination, voluntarism, common contribution and shared benefits, and respect for the United Nations Charter and international laws" (LMC 2016: para. 11). These cooperative principles and the future direction of the LMC Mechanism was elaborated upon and reinforced in January 2018 with the release of the Phnom Penh Declaration at the Second LMC Leader's Meeting (LMC 2018). In spite of its quick development (Devlaeminck 2019), it remains to be seen how these latest developments and the resulting cooperative framework will unfold. This progress, however, clearly illustrates that China is more interested in working with its riparian neighbours and recognizing the interests of its neighbours, than forging ahead on its own.

Future development of the law of international watercourses: The community of interests and China's "community of common destiny"

As international law has developed, it has become gripped by the need to support universal moral beliefs while also reflecting its political context (Simma 1994). Reciprocity is often associated with the bilateral context, and thus Paulus notes that

> if the obligation is strictly reciprocal between the states parties, reciprocity applies. If, however, the provision also serves the more general interest of the international community, or it benefits other, third persons, it goes beyond the bilateral relationship between parties and thereby also beyond reciprocity.
>
> (Paulus 2011: 119)

As international law develops and moves from a system where bilateral relations between sovereign states are key, and one which aims to include and protect fundamental human values within the body of international law (Simma 1994), the importance of reciprocity is likely to change as well.

The development of the law of international watercourses first began as primarily bilateral relationships, which were often facilitated by reciprocation between parties. However, as it has developed it too has witnessed the insertion of fundamental values, for example, through the development of the human right to water, but also through the development of a fourth primary principle, the community of interests. Derived from the natural unity of watercourses (McCaffrey 2019), cooperation within the framework of the community of interests may contain one or more of the following five elements:

1) a promotion of a drainage approach;
2) a view of watercourses as common property;
3) mutual consent;
4) joint management of the shared water resources; and
5) basin or sub-basin agreements and institutions.

(Rocha Loures 2015)

The community of interests can be viewed as reinforcing claims of limited territorial sovereignty (McCaffrey 2019), but it could also be said that it transcends sovereignty since states are members of the community due to their shared hydrologic system (Leb 2013). As such, the community of interests may transcend reciprocity as we know it; however, given that this theory is relatively underdeveloped, the role that reciprocity will play is unclear.

Reciprocity is likely to play a role in the development of the community of interests, but once such a community has been established the role of reciprocity may move "from the master to the slave" (Paulus 2011: 115). As cooperation continues through concessions in good faith followed by reciprocation states are able to identify their common interests, thus assisting with the formation of the community of interests. As the community of interests "evokes the necessity of cooperation to ensure that competing interests do not stand in the way of one another" (Leb 2013: 53), such cooperation will be pushed forward by the common interests of riparians, not reciprocal exchange. Although this may be the case, reciprocity will not disappear, but will remain an important factor in enforcement. Treaties established under a community of interests act as a "reciprocal promise" between states, since each state has an interest in the treaty being upheld by all parties (Paulus 2011: 126). If states violate a rule within a community of interest then its community members may be permitted to reciprocate in order to bring that state back into line, discussed further in Chapter 5. Even if reciprocity will not be a prime mover within the community of interests, it is too early to say that its role in the development of law will be lost since such enforcement can also act as a mechanism of the development of law.

A community of interests approach may be emerging within China's state practice through the development of the "community of common destiny," broadly defined as a "group of people/nations bonded together by common interest and fate" (Zhang 2017: 197). As a new concept of China's state diplomacy, the community of common destiny finds its roots in interdependence, sustainable development and common interests (Zeng 2016). China has not offered a clear definition, but has elaborated on the concept in its public statements. At the 2013 Boao Forum, noting that humanity shared one earth, Xi Jinping stated that "common development, which is the very foundation of sustainable development, serves the long-term and fundamental interests of all the people in the world" (Xi 2013). He further elaborated upon the concept at the 2015 Boao Forum, where President Xi stated that "to build a community of common destiny, we need to seek win–win cooperation and common development" (Xi 2015b). Such an approach, as illustrated at the 2015 Asia–Africa Summit, entails that "cooperation must be based on equality without which there would be no win–win cooperation," and that "all countries, big or small, strong or weak, rich or poor, are all equal embers of the international community entitled to equal participation in regional and international affairs" (Xi 2015a). In order to construct this community, China will need to establish political partnerships, and promote security, economic development, cultural exchange and the environment (Zhang 2017). The LMC Mechanism exemplifies this language as it loosely displays aspects of the community of interests approach, recognizing the interconnectivity of Lancang-Mekong states indicating they are "six countries linked by mountains and rivers" (LMC 2016: preamble). It, however, remains unclear if this will take on greater aspects of a community of interests as it develops, or whether it merely represents a change in the language surrounding China's approach to state relations via the Five Principles.

Conclusion

This chapter has outlined the development of international law in regards to sovereignty claims, from absolute territorial sovereignty and absolute territorial integrity to limited territorial sovereignty and beyond to the community of interests. Throughout its development, reciprocity and the influence that it has on state claims has had a significant impact on the norms of customary law that have emerged in the field. As a prime mover within the international legal system, expectations of reciprocity and legal reciprocity have worked to determine and maintain the balance we find today between states, and, in the law of international watercourses, establishing limited territorial sovereignty as customary international law. This norm, requiring states to take each other's interests into consideration in a reciprocal manner, acts as the foundation for the law of international watercourses providing the grounds for substantive rules of equitable and reasonable use and the due diligence obligation not to cause significant harm, discussed further in the next chapter. Although some may perceive limited territorial sovereignty to be a theory of altruism, the process of reciprocity illustrates that, at best, it is based upon enlightened self-interest. With its roots in the push and pull between upstream and downstream states based on concerns for their domestic economies and environment, this is not surprising.

As an "upstream superpower" (Nickum 2008: 227) seeking to develop its transboundary waters, it is not surprising that China has encountered criticism and mistrust, particularly as it is often the case that China's downstream neighbours are more vulnerable than upstream China to geopolitical and environmental hazards (Kattelus et al. 2015). It has been argued, however, that China's practice, in one way or another, reflects absolute territorial sovereignty. A closer look at China's legal practice indicates, however, that at the *legal level* China clearly does not practice absolute territorial sovereignty. In a dissenting opinion to the *Customs Regime Case*, it is stated that "practically, every treaty entered into between independent States restricts to some extent the exercise of the power incidental to sovereignty. Complete and absolute sovereignty unrestricted by any obligations imposed by treaties is impossible and practically unknown" (PCIJ 1931: 44). With a series of treaties and agreements concerning China's transboundary waters that shape and contour their state interactions, it is clear that China practices some form of limited territorial sovereignty, recognizing that it cannot develop unilaterally without consideration for the needs and interests of its neighbours. Some states may be in a position to act as a persistent objector, but the broad nature of reciprocal exchange, as well as the desire to maintain a good reputation, can lead even powerful states, like China, to cooperate.

As the fulcrum of cooperation shifts from national sovereigns to global communities (Wouters & Tarlock 2013), the role of reciprocity will be altered but not abandoned. As states move towards closer and deeper cooperation based on common interest, reciprocity will no longer be a prime mover, but it is unlikely to disappear entirely as the international system continues to have sovereign states at its centre without a central authority. As such, reciprocity is likely to assist in the further development of these norms, and continue to act as a mechanism of enforcement. As cooperation grows and China seeks to establish a community of common destiny amongst itself and its neighbours through joint development initiatives, most notably the Belt and Road Initiative, China's legal practice may be moving beyond the typical reciprocal framework to recognize greater normative imperatives. Reminiscent of the community of interests doctrine, China's community of common destiny may set the normative framework for future interactions and cooperative river development between China and its neighbours. This would best be done, however, through the norms and rules set out in the global water conventions.

Acknowledgements

A version of this chapter first appeared as an article in the *Journal of Water Law*. For the original article, see Devlaeminck, D. (2016). Reciprocity and the Development of International Water Law, *Journal of Water Law 25*, 80–7. Retrieved from www.lawtext.com/lawtextweb/default.jsp?PageID=2. Sections of this chapter also appeared in the *Chinese Journal of Environmental Law*. For the original article, see Devlaeminck, D. J. (2018). The Legal Principle of Reciprocity and China's Water Treaty Practice. *Chinese Journal of Environmental Law, 2*(2), 195–222.

Notes

1 At the time, a British company was planning the construction of a dam on the river within USA territory. The USA revoked its construction permit, claiming that the official who had provided it was not authorized to do so, and sued the company under the pretence that the dam would "seriously obstruct the navigable capacity of the said river." A dam was then constructed at Engle, which was to fulfil its obligation to Mexico in the resolution of this dispute, even though it was not the dam that was proposed (McCaffrey 1996).

2 Read opined that if the case required the complete cessation of pollution that the use of land on either side of the border for industrial or urban purposes would be impossible. He stated that "the householder in Detroit or Buffalo or Niagara Falls cannot light a fire in his kitchen stove without contributing to a smoke cloud which may drift across the river to Ontario and cause damage" (Read 1963: 224–5).

3 Although China is discussed here, India is also a good example of an upstream regional power that also appears to recognize the rights of its downstream neighbours. During the conflict prior to the signing of the 1960 Indus Waters Treaty, India made claims of absolute territorial sovereignty. The rights of downstream Pakistan, however, were recognized within the treaty and the waters were divided equally between the two parties. This is most likely an instance where absolute territorial sovereignty was used as a tool of negotiation, and does not reflect the legal obligations states believe they must follow (McCaffrey 2019). It has been argued, however, that Turkey, an upstream power, claims absolute territorial sovereignty within its domestic law and has opposed international initiatives such as the Watercourses Convention. Although it claims absolute territorial sovereignty, it recognizes equitable and reasonable use and no-significant harm within domestic legislation (Zeitoun 2015).

4 In 2016 the Permanent Court of Arbitration ruled against China in a case brought to it by the Philippines. Although the ruling has not been strictly upheld, it is clear, however, that China has not entirely ignored the ruling and may have "tempered" its actions or aimed towards a "stealthy compliance" in the South China Sea (Welch 2017).

References

Adeel, Z., Aslov, S., Maestu, J. & Unver, O. (2015). *Water Cooperation: Views on Progress and the Way Forward*. UNU-INWEH. Retrieved from http://inweh.unu.edu/portfolio/water-cooperation-views-progress-way-forward/

Byers, M. (2004). *Custom, Power and the Power of Rules: International Relations and Customary Law*. Cambridge: Cambridge University Press.

Chellaney, B. (2013). *Water, Peace and War: Confronting the Global Water Crisis.* Lanham: Rowman and Littlefield Press.

Chen, H., Rieu-Clarke, A. & Wouters, P. (2013). Exploring China's Transboundary Water Treaty Practice Through the Prism of the UN Watercourses Convention. *Water International, 38*(2), 217–30.

China–Kazakhstan (2001). Agreement on Cooperation in the Use and Protection of Transboundary Rivers (signed February 22, 2001).

Crawford, J. (2012). *Brownlie's Principles of Public International Law* (8 ed.). Oxford: Oxford University Press.

Crawford, J. (2015). Responsibility, Fraternity and Sustainability in International Law. *Canadian Yearbook of International Law, 52*, 1–34.

Devlaeminck, D. J. (2019). Timeline of the Lancang-Mekong Cooperation (LMC) Mechanism. *Academia.edu.* Retrieved from https://davidjdevlaeminck.com/research-resource

Devlaeminck, D. J., Wouters, P. & Yang, L. (2020). List of China's Transboundary Water Agreements and Related Documents. *Academia.edu.* Retrieved from https://davidjdevlaeminck.com/research-resource

Dinar, S. (2008). *International Water Treaties: Negotiation and Cooperation Along Transboundary Rivers.* London/New York: Routledge.

Fard, S. N. (2016). *Reciprocity in International Law: Its Impact and Function.* London/New York: Routledge.

Gouldner, A. W. (1960). The Norm of Reciprocity: A Preliminary Statement. *American Sociological Review, 25*(2), 161–78.

Green, J. A. (2016). *The Persistent Objector Rule in International Law.* Oxford: Oxford University Press.

Guzman, A. T. (2008). *How International Law Works: A Rational Choice Theory.* Oxford: Oxford University Press.

Han, H. (2017). China, An Upstream Hegemon: A Destabilizer for the Governance of the Mekong River? *Pacific Focus, XXXII*(1), 30–55.

Ho, S. (2017). China's Transboundary River Policies Towards Kazakhstan: Issue-Linkages and Incentives for Cooperation *Water International, 42*(2), 142–62.

ICJ (1945). Statute of the International Court of Justice (adopted October 24, 1945).

ICJ (1986). Case Concerning Military and Paramilitary Activities in and Against Nicaragua (Nicaragua V. United States of America) – Judgement, (International Court of Justice, June 27, 1986).

ICJ (1997). Case Concerning the Gabčíkovo-Nagymaros Project (Hungary v. Slovakia) – Judgement, (International Court of Justice, September 25, 1997).

ICJ (2010). Case Concerning Pulp Mills on the River Uruguay (Argentina v. Uruguay) – Judgement, (International Court of Justice, April 20, 2010).

IJC (1941). Trail Smelter Case (United States of America v. Canada) (International Joint Commission, April 16, 1938 and March 11, 1941).

ILA (1966). The Helsinki Rules on the Uses of the Waters of International Rivers (adopted August 1966).

ILC (2018). Draft Conclusions on Identification of Customary International Law with Commentaries (A/73/10). Retrieved from https://legal.un.org/ilc/texts/instruments/english/commentaries/1_13_2018.pdf

Kattelus, M., Kummu, M., Keskinen, M., Samlivaara, A. & Varis, O. (2015). China's Southbound Transboundary River Basins: A Case of Asymmetry. *Water International, 40*(1), 113–38.

Keohane, R. O. (1986). Reciprocity in International Relations. *International Organization, 40*(1), 1–27.

Klein, E. (2011). Denunciation of Human Rights Treaties and the Principle of Reciprocity. In R. G. Ulrich Fastenrath, Daniel-Erasmus Khan, Andreas Paulus, Sabine von Schorlemer & Christoph Vedder (Eds.), *From Bilateralism to Community Interest: Essays in Honour of Bruno Simma.* Oxford: Oxford University Press.

Leb, C. (2013). *Cooperation in the Law of Transboundary Water Resources.* Cambridge: Cambridge University Press.

Leb, C. (2014). One Step at a Time: International Law and the Duty to Cooperate in the Management of Shared Water Resources. *Water International, 40*(1), 21–32.

Lee, S. (2015). Benefit Sharing in the Mekong River Basin. *Water International, 40*(1), 139–52.

Liebman, A. (2005). Trickle-down Hegemony?: China's "Peaceful Rise" and Dam Building on the Mekong. *Contemporary Southeast Asia: A Journal of Strategic Affairs, 27*(2), 281–304.

LMC (2016). Sanya Declaration of the First Lancang-Mekong Cooperation (LMC) Leaders' Meeting (adopted March 23, 2016).

LMC (2018). Phnom Penh Declaration of the Second Lancang-Mekong Cooperation (LMC) Leaders' Meeting (adopted January 10, 2018).

McCaffrey, S. (1996). The Harmon Doctrine One Hundred Years Later: Buried, Not Praised. *Natural Resources Journal, 36*(4), 549–90.

McCaffrey, S. (2019). *The Law of International Watercourses* (3 ed.). Oxford: Oxford University Press.

McIntyre, O. (2007). *Environmental Protection of International Watercourses under International Law*, Aldershot/Burlington: Ashgate Publishing.

Menniken, T. (2007). China's Performance in International Resource Politics: Lessons from the Mekong. *Contemporary Southeast Asia: A Journal of Strategic Affairs, 29*(1), 97–120.

Mexico–USA (1906). Convention between the United States and Mexico: Equitable Distribution of the Waters of the Rio Grande (signed May 21, 1906).

MFA (2016a). China's National Plan on Implementation of the 2030 Agenda for Sustainable Development. *Ministry of Foreign Affairs of the People's Republic of China.* Retrieved from www.fmprc.gov.cn/mfa_eng/zxxx_662805/W020161014332600482185.pdf

MFA (2016b). Five Features of Lancang-Mekong River Cooperation. *Ministry of Foreign Affairs of the People's Republic of China.* Retrieved from www.fmprc.gov.cn/mfa_eng/zxxx_662805/t1349239.shtml

Mickelson, K. (1993). Rereading the Trail Smelter. *Canadian Yearbook of International Law, 31*, 219–34.

Molm, L. D. (2010). The Structure of Reciprocity. *Social Psychology Quarterly, 73*(2), 119–31.

Mushkat, R. (2011). State Reputation and Compliance with International Law: Looking through a Chinese Lens. *Chinese Journal of International Law, 10*, 703–37.

Nickum, J. E. (2008). The Upstream Superpower: China's International Rivers. In O. Varis, A. Biswas & C. Tortajada (Eds.), *Management of Transboundary Rivers and Lakes* (pp. 227–44). Berlin-Heidelberg: Springer.

Patchen, M. (1998). When Does Reciprocity in the Actions of Nations Occur? *International Negotiations, 3*, 171–96.

Paulus, A. (2011). Reciprocity Revisited. In R. G. Ulrich Fastenrath, Daniel-Erasmus Khan, Andreas Paulus, Sabine von Schorlemer, Christoph Vedder (Ed.), *From Bilateralism to Community Interest: Essays in Honour of Bruno Simma* (pp. 114–37). Oxford: Oxford University Press.

PCIJ (1931). Customs Regime between Germany and Austria (Protocol of March 19, 1931) (Germany v. Austria) – Dissenting Opinion of M. Adatci, Mr. Kellogg, Baron Rolin-Jaequemyns, Sir Cecil Hurst, M. Schuking, Jonkheer Van Eysinga and M. Wang (Permanent Court of International Justice, September 5, 1931).

Ptak, T. & Hommel, D. (2016). The Trans-Political Nature of Southwest China's Energy Conduit, Yunnan Province. *Geopolitics, 21*(3), 556–78.

Read, J. E. (1963). The Trail Smelter Dispute. *Canadian Yearbook of International Law, 1*, 213–29.

Rocha Loures, F. (2015). The Dragon as Part of Transboundary Basin "Villages": Community of Interests and International Law in China. *Journal of Water Law, 24*, 220–38.

Simma, B. (1994). From Bilateralism to Community Interest. *Recueil des Cours, 250*, 217–387.

Simma, B. (2008). Reciprocity. In R. Wolfrum (Ed.), *Max Planck Encyclopedias of International Law*, Oxford: Oxford University Press.

Su, Y. (2014). Contemporary Legal Analysis of China's Transboundary Water Regimes: International Law in Practice. *Water International, 39*(5), 705–24.

UNGA (2015). *Transforming our World: The 2030 Agenda for Sustainable Development*, A/RES/70/1 (October 21, 2015). Retrieved from www.un.org/ga/search/view_doc.asp?symbol=A/RES/70/1&Lang=E

UNU-INWEH (2016). Water Cycle Instability is Here to Stay Posing Major Political and Economic Risks: UN Experts. *EurekAlert* – April 4. Retrieved from www.eurekalert.org/pub_releases/2016-04/tca-wci040316.php

VCLT (1969). Vienna Convention on the Law of Treaties (adopted May 23, 1969; entered into force January 27, 1980).

Wang, T. (1990). International Law in China: Historical and Contemporary Perspectives. *Recueil de Cours, 221*, 195–368.

Water Convention (1992). Convention on the Protection and Use of Transboundary Watercourses and International Lakes (adopted on March 17, 1992; entered into force October 6, 1996).

Watercourses Convention (1997). United Nations Convention on the Law of Non-Navigational Uses of International Watercourses (adopted on May 21, 1997; entered into force August 17, 2014).

Welch, D. (2017). Philippines v. China One Year Later: A Surprising Compliance From Beijing. *The Globe and Mail* – July 12. Retrieved from www.theglobeandmail.com/opinion/philippines-v-china-one-year-later-a-surprising-compliance-from-beijing/article35660244//

Wirth, J. D. (1996). The Trail Smelter Dispute: Canadians and Americans Confront Transboundary Pollution. *Environmental History, 1*(2), 34–51.

Wouters, P. (2014). The Yin and Yang of International Water Law: China's Transboundary Water Practice and the Changing Contours of Sovereignty. *RECIEL, 23*(1), 67–75.

Wouters, P. & Chen, H. (2013). China's "Soft-Path" to Transboundary Water Cooperation Examined in the Light of Two UN Global Water Conventions – Exploring the "Chinese Way." *Journal of Water Law, 22*(6), 229–47.

Wouters, P. & Tarlock, A. D. (2013). The Third Wave of Normativity in Global Water Law: The Duty to Cooperate in the Peaceful Management of the World's Water Resources: An Emerging Obligation Erga Omnes? *Journal of Water Law, 23*, 51–65.

Xi, J. (2013). Working Together Toward a Better Future for Asia and the World, Keynote Speech, Boao Forum for Asia. Retrieved from http://english.boaoforum.org/mtzxxwzxen/7379.jhtml

Xi, J. (2015a). Carry Forward the Bandung Spirit for Win-Win Cooperation: Remarks by Chinese President Xi Jinping *Ministry of Foreign Affairs of the People's Republic of China.* Retrieved from www.fmprc.gov.cn/mfa_eng/wjdt_665385/zyjh_665391/t1259844.shtml

Xi, J. (2015b). Towards a Community of Common Destiny and a New Future for Asia, Keynote Speech, Boao Forum for Asia Annual Conference. Retrieved from http://news.xinhuanet.com/english/2015-03/29/c_134106145.htm

Xi, J. (2015c). Towards Win-Win Partnership for Sustainable Development – Remarks by H.E. Xi Jinping President of the People's Republic of China at the United Nations Sustainable Development Summit. Retrieved from https://sustainabledevelopment.un.org/content/documents/20548china.pdf

Zeitoun, M. (2015). The Relevance of International Water Law to Later-Developing Upstream States. *Water International, 40*(7), 949–68.

Zeng, L. (2016). Conceptual Analysis of China's Belt and Road Initiative: A Road Towards a Regional Community of Common Destiny. *Chinese Journal of International Law, 15*, 517–41.

Zhang, D. (2017). The Concept of "Community of Common Destiny" in China's Diplomacy: Meaning, Motives and Implications. *Asia & the Pacific Policy Studies, 5*(2), 196–207.

4 Revisiting the substantive rules of the law of international watercourses

Adopted in 1966, the Helsinki Rules (ILA 1966) acted as the "first general codification of the law of international watercourse" (Salman 2007a: 630), incorporating the notion of limited territorial sovereignty through the inclusion of the principle of equitable and reasonable use. While the Helsinki Rules are not legally binding upon states, they "remained the single most authoritative and widely quoted set of rules for regulating the use and protection of international watercourses" (Salman 2007a: 630) until the drafting and adoption of the two global water conventions concerning the law of international watercourses, the 1997 United Nations Convention on the Law of the Non-navigational Uses of International Watercourses (Watercourses Convention) and the 1992 United Nations Economic Commission for Europe (UNECE) Convention on the Protection and Use of Transboundary Watercourses and International Lakes (Water Convention).

In 1970, "considering that water, owing to the growth of population and the increasing and multiplying needs and demands of mankind is a growing concern to humanity," the United Nations (UN) Sixth Committee recommended that the International Law Commission (ILC) "take up the study of the law of the non-navigational uses of international watercourses" (UNGA 1970). The process, lasting 27 years, resulted in the adoption of the Watercourses Convention in 1997, which aims to codify and develop the rules and practice that govern the law of international watercourses. Although the Watercourses Convention received wide support at the United Nations General Assembly (UNGA) with 106 votes in favour, 3 against, and 22 abstentions, it entered into force after nearly 17 years in August 2014 (UNTC 1997). The earlier Water Convention, which also incorporates the rules of equitable and reasonable use and the due diligence obligation not to cause significant harm as its normative foundation, was the result of a much shorter drafting process and, as of 2013, is now open for accession globally.

There are multiple reasons why the Watercourses Convention had taken so long to enter into force, but one of the primary reasons relates to contention surrounding two of its primary principles: equitable and reasonable use, and the due diligence obligation not to cause significant harm. Citing an imbalance in the rights and duties and perceived favouritism of these principles for either upstream or downstream riparians, some states, including China, did not support it and voted against the Convention. It should be clearly stated, however, that a vote against does not necessarily mean that China opposes the norms set out in the Convention, and multiple authors have pointed out that the primary norms of the global water conventions are evident in China's water treaty practice (Chen et al. 2013; Su 2014, 2019; Wouters 2014; Wouters & Chen 2013), and even reflected in its domestic water law (Fry & Chong 2016). Why then did China vote against the Convention and why has it not made moves to accede to either of the global water conventions since? China cited four reasons for its vote against adoption of the draft of the Convention: 1) it did not represent a general agreement by all countries, 2) it did not reflect a state's sovereignty over the parts of a watercourse which flows through a state's territory, 3) a preference to choose the method of dispute settlement, and most importantly for this chapter, 4) a perceived imbalance between upstream and downstream states (UNGA 1997a). China was not alone in this sentiment, and many other states shared this perception. As the water crisis continues to escalate and is further exacerbated by climate change, recent studies have illustrated that these tensions continue to hinder the engagement of states (primarily upstream) with the global water conventions (Eckstein 2020), linking such concerns to reciprocity (Zhong et al. 2016). It is within treaties where reciprocity plays its most vital role, informing the distribution of rights and duties, advantages and disadvantages. Such reciprocal distribution brings a sense of fairness, further promoting the sovereign equality of states. Reminiscent of the tension between absolute territorial sovereignty and absolute territorial integrity, upstream states have often favoured equitable and reasonable use, whereas downstream states have often favoured the duty not to cause significant harm, both perceiving these rules to provide protection for their uses. In spite of these perceptions, an analysis through the lens of reciprocity illustrates that these principles establish a fair balance of corresponding rights and duties, protecting the interests of both upstream and downstream states, providing clarity at a time when both the Watercourses Convention and Water Convention are open for accession to all states.

This chapter will analyse the substantive norms of the global water conventions through the lens of reciprocity, aiming to illustrate that they are balanced and capable of protecting the interests of both upstream and downstream states, while also illustrating that China's transboundary water treaty practice follows a similar approach. In order to conduct this analysis, this chapter will first discuss the role that reciprocity plays in various kinds of treaties and treaty obligations. This chapter will then turn to analyse the global water conventions as well as the Berlin Rules, which provide a notable alternative arrangement between the substantive rules. Beginning with the Watercourses Convention, it will first set the stage for its analysis, exploring its drafting process including a review of relevant state views, especially China, illustrating that the perception of the Convention as imbalanced or favours states in certain geographic positions while putting others at a disadvantage is widespread. Given that aspects of the Watercourses Convention are often considered to be a codification of customary law, the principle of equitable and reasonable use (1997: art. 5 & 6) as well as the duty not to cause significant harm (1997: art. 7) found within the Convention will then be analysed through the lens of reciprocity. China, as a non-UNECE member state, did not participate in the drafting process and this contention was not evident in the drafting process of the Water Convention, which was "conducted efficiently and effectively" taking less than two years (Rieu-Clarke 2015: 12). Even so, the chapter will turn to an analysis of the substantive rules found within the Water Convention. This will be followed by an analysis of the relationship between these two principles in the Berlin Rules (2004), an attempt by the International Law Association (ILA) to update the Helsinki Rules, which follow a very different reciprocal structure. Although reciprocity is prominent in the substantive rules of the law of international watercourses, certain emerging aspects of these rules may not follow this reciprocal structure. As such, the chapter will discuss the humanization and environmentalization of the law of international watercourses, as well as its influence on China's treaty practice. The chapter will conclude with a discussion of river basin organizations (RBOs) and benefit-sharing as methods to institutionalize the reciprocity at the core of the global water conventions and to enhance opportunities for balance in the rights and obligations of riparians.

Reciprocity in treaties: reciprocating and non-reciprocating provisions

As trust builds and states meet their good faith and reciprocal obligations, ties between them increase, and given states' desire for stable and predictable relationships, these interactions are often formalized within treaties (Leb 2014). It is in treaties where reciprocity arguably plays its most important role, as international law provides a "reciprocity based framework [...] for legal transactions in the form of treaties" (Simma 1994: 224). In its legal form, reciprocity establishes corresponding rights and duties between parties in which the right of one is the duty of the other (Simma 1989), and thus treaties act as a "reciprocal arrangement which determine the rights and obligations of the parties" (Fard 2016: 20). In this role, reciprocity works to inform the distribution of advantages and disadvantages, rights and obligations, promoting balance and a sense of fairness within the treaty regime. Reciprocity "governs every international agreement, independent of its content" (Simma 2008: para. 4), and as a reflection of the formal aspects of reciprocity any treaty could be considered reciprocal since every state party is "legally entitled to expect compliance from the other parties, and vice versa" (Paulus 2011: 117). In terms of legal reciprocity, however, not all treaty provisions involve such "reciprocal arrangements," and can be broadly classified into classes of reciprocating and non-reciprocating provisions (Fitzmaurice 1958: 27).

Reciprocating treaty provisions

Bilateral treaties are those international agreements concluded between only two states, and provisions within bilateral treaties often involve aspects of reciprocity, or *quid pro quo* (Byers 2004). For example, Article 22 of the 1961 Vienna Convention on the Law of Diplomatic Relations (VCDR), which provides protection for diplomatic missions of one country on the foreign soil of another, exemplifies a bilateral relationship between two states with corresponding rights and duties (VCDR 1961). States have an interest in protecting the foreign missions of other states based on reciprocity in the sense that a state takes on the duty to protect and respect another state's mission within their sovereign territory and in return the other state will do the same for their missions within their territory. Furthermore, violation of that right will permit the state whose mission was not protected to act against the state who failed to protect it.

Multilateral treaties involve more than two parties, but they too can be conceptualized as "bundles" of bilateral obligations, often connected through a multilateral instrument (Pauwelyn 2003: 908; Simma 1989). Given that the aforementioned VCDR is multilateral, Article 22 also exemplifies a multilateral obligation that can be broken down into bundles of bilateral relations. Parties to the Convention consent to the duty to protect foreign missions on their soil to all other parties of the Convention. For example, state A has the bilateral duty to both state B and C, state B has the duty to A and C and so on. This duty, however, remains bilateral in the sense that the relationship between two parties can be detached from the others. If state A were to have their right violated by state B, then A, and only A, can act against B, and only B. These bundles of bilateral obligations can also be seen in the regime of state reservations to treaties, as set out in the 1969 Vienna Convention on the Law of Treaties, Article 19–23 (VCLT 1969). States consent to treaties through accession and subsequent signature and ratification; however, they are also able to place reservations on select sections of the treaty so long as reservations are not prohibited or limited by the treaty in question, and said reservations are compatible "with the object and purpose of the treaty" (VCLT 1969: art. 19). Such reservations ensure that they will not be bound by that specific provision, and "enable states to limit their obligations but still be part of the treaty," permitting states to reach consensus (Fard 2016: 21). In practice, however, states often make minimal reservations, since such reservations place reciprocal limitations on the duties between state parties. Therefore, if one state makes a reservation to a provision which establishes a right or duty upon it, this limits the corresponding right or duty of the other parties in relation to that state (Fard 2016); however, the corresponding right/duty persists between the other parties. Thus, if state A makes a reservation to a treaty provision, then B and C do not owe state A the corresponding right, but the right/duty persists between state B and C.

Reciprocity within treaties emerges from the "actual equivalence of mutual advantages deriving from treaty performance" (Simma 2008: para. 4).

Such equivalence brings a sense of fairness into the rules,[1] given that "a perception of the fairness of any particular rule depends, in major part, on its implicit promise to treat like with like" (Franck 1995: 10). Reciprocity as a treaty mechanism, however, would not be possible without the principles of *pacta sunt servanda* and good faith, both of which are universally recognized. *Pacta sunt servanda* entails that "every treaty in force is binding upon the parties and it must be performed by them in good faith" (VCLT 1969: art. 26). Good faith, which is "the basis of trust and thus the essence of cooperation within a society of States" (Leb 2013: 32), requires states to perform their treaty obligations based on "honesty, reasonableness and fairness" (Fard 2016: 25). As decided in the *North Sea Continental Shelf Case*, acting in good faith requires states to conduct themselves in such a way that "negotiations are meaningful, which will not be the case when either of them insists upon its own position without contemplating any modification of it" (ICJ 1969: para. 85). Together these principles establish consistency within the interpretation of the law, promoting fairness and ultimately providing the foundation upon which reciprocity can be applied. This ultimately discourages states from interpreting the rules in such a way as to provide them with an advantage (Fard 2016). The inclusion of such reciprocal rights and obligations within treaties is one way in which the effective implementation of a treaty can be ensured (Simma 2008) since the reciprocal interest of states to uphold such duties is one of the primary reasons for their effectiveness, providing stability to the system (Leb 2013).

Non-reciprocating treaty provisions

A system based on bilateral reciprocal relations, however, is often criticized for standing in the way of greater international solidarity (Simma 1994). With the evolution of the international legal system, however, more and more overarching values have been inserted into treaties. Such areas of "community interest" rely upon a "consensus according to which respect for certain fundamental values is not to be left to the free disposition of States individually or *inter se* but is recognized and sanctioned by the law as a matter of concern to all States" (Simma 1989: 823). Thus, not all treaties or treaty provisions can be broken down into bundles of bilateral rights and duties. This is often the case in environmental agreements, which are born out of the collective interests of states[2] and not the individual interests of state parties (Pauwelyn 2003). Environmental agreements, connecting areas that have been artificially divided by state borders, essentially require states to agree to unilateral obligations (Bodansky 2010; Brunée 1989). These unilateral obligations are carried out within their own territory, and thus do not establish a form of reciprocal exchange between the parties (Simma 1989). For example, as discussed in Chapter 2, it could be argued that reciprocity plays no role in many of the provisions of the UN Framework Convention on Climate Change since the duties are largely owed to the international community as a whole, and not to individual states (Mehling 2012). In these treaties, however, states do have a reciprocal interest in all contracting parties upholding their rights under the treaty and contributing to the overall goal of such a treaty (Brunée 1989; Simma 2008). Thus, reciprocity and collective interests coincide in the sense that states have an interest in "not being impaired by equal conduct of another state" (Brunée 1989: 807).

Perceived balance and imbalance in the Watercourses Convention

The Watercourses Convention has had a lengthy process of development, negotiation, and eventually, ratification, finally entering into force in August 2014. Many authors cite different reasons why this may have been the case, including treaty congestion, a lack of awareness and capacity and a lack of champions for the Convention (Dellapenna et al. 2013; Rieu-Clarke & Loures 2009). However, there were also many areas of contention concerning various treaty provisions, including the notification process under the Convention, the way in which the Convention does or does not apply to existing agreements, whether or not the dispute settlement provisions of the Convention are too weak or too strong, the "expanded definition" of the term "Watercourses State," and concern over the loss of sovereignty surrounding international watercourses (Salman 2007b: 8–12). Most importantly for this discussion, however, was concern surrounding the relationship between the principles of equitable and reasonable use (1997: art. 5 & 6) and the duty not to cause significant harm (1997: art. 7), which together provide the foundation for a cooperative framework on transboundary waters. Some states, however, argued that the principle of equitable and reasonable use favours upstream riparians, whereas the duty not to cause significant harm favours downstream states, as was evident during the drafting process of the Watercourses Convention at the UN 6th Committee. China's statements at these meetings clearly reflect the concern that these provisions are imbalanced towards states in different positions, while illustrating its desire for a balance of rights and obligations. Given that China is primarily an upstream country with a strong stance on state sovereignty and a preference for bilateral agreements with its riparians, reciprocity will arguably play a strong role in its transboundary water cooperation. Thus, it is not surprising that it would strive for greater balance in these provisions. China, however, is certainly not alone in this regard.

At the 12th Meeting of the 6th Committee China had stated its support for the Watercourses Convention Draft Articles, stating that they "represented a realistic, balanced approach to the need to reconcile the different interests of watercourse States" (UNGA 1996a: para. 42). Furthermore, at the 15th and 17th meetings the Chinese delegation stated that both Article 5 and Article 7 represented a balance between the rights and obligations of upstream and downstream states (UNGA 1996b; 1996c). With the introduction of a new draft at the 51st meeting, however, China's support began to waver, and its opinion of these articles changed. At the 61st meeting, taking Articles 5, 6 and 7 as a whole, many states argued that these provisions were balanced (Argentina, Brazil, Chile, Egypt, Hungary, Mexico, Portugal, Republic of Korea, Romania and Vietnam) whereas others argued that the balance had been upset (Austria, China, Czech Republic, Ethiopia, India, Israel, Liechtenstein, Slovakia, Syrian Arab Republic and Turkey) (UNGA 1997b) – see Table 4.1.

While many of the states who claimed it was balanced voted in favour (Brazil, Chile, Hungary, Mexico, Portugal, Republic of Korea, Romania and Vietnam) and a select few of those who claimed it was imbalanced voted against (China and Turkey), these categories do not always line up so neatly. Argentina and Egypt claimed this relationship was balanced, while Ethiopia, Czech Republic, India and Slovakia stated it was somehow imbalanced, but all abstained. Austria, Israel, and Liechtenstein, and Syria stated it was somehow imbalanced, but voted in favour of the draft (UNGA 1997c). The Chinese delegation stated that these provisions "were the cornerstone of the convention and should reflect a balance between rights and obligations," however, they believed that the text, which was a compromise between various interests, "failed to strike a balance between rights and obligations" (UNGA 1997b: para. 14). At the 62nd meeting China could not support the draft treaty since it "did not resolve the imbalance between upstream and downstream states" (UNGA 1997c: para. 6). When before the UNGA, China was one of three states to vote against the resolution, reaffirming its belief that in "the draft Conventions provisions regarding the rights and obligations of States there is an obvious imbalance between those of States on the upper reaches of an international watercourse and those of States on the lower reaches" (UNGA 1997a: 6).

China's statements during the drafting process illustrate that some states believed the rules could be interpreted in such a way as to favour upstream or downstream riparians. This is supported by recent studies which illustrate that downstream riparians tended to vote in favour of the Watercourses Convention, whereas upstream states tended to abstain or vote against it, further linking this to a misunderstanding of the reciprocal nature of the Convention (Eckstein 2020; Zhong et al. 2016). As a reincarnation of the clash between absolute territorial sovereignty and absolute territorial integrity, this divide has been connected to geographical considerations. Upstream states favoured equitable and reasonable use since it *appears* to provide space for them to utilize their waters in ways that may impact their downstream neighbours. Downstream states, however, preferred the duty not to cause significant harm since it *appears* to provide protection against impacts from upstream activities (Salman 2007b). Such interpretations, although incorrect, would benefit their competing interests, given that downstream states often develop first due to flatter, more suitable terrain, whereas the typically more mountainous terrain of upstream states often requires more advanced technology prior to development (McCaffrey 2014). Recent studies of the voting record appear to confirm this, indicating that upstream states have tended not to engage with the

Table 4.1 Select state comments concerning the perceived balance or imbalance of the Watercourses Convention

State	*Comment at the 61st Meeting*	*Draft Vote*	*UNGA Vote*	*Party status*	
				UNWC	*UNECE*
Argentina	Balanced: "the Chairman's proposal was balanced and that they were prepared to accept it in order to facilitate a consensus."	Abstain	Abstain		
Austria	Imbalanced: "since articles 5 and 7 were the cornerstones of the convention, it was crucial to have a balanced text. Austria could not join in a consensus on articles 5 and 7 [...]."	In Favour	In Favour		X
Brazil	Balanced: "the Chairman's proposal was balanced and that they were prepared to accept it in order to facilitate a consensus."	In Favour	In Favour		
Chile	Balanced: "the Chairman's proposal was balanced and that they were prepared to accept it in order to facilitate a consensus."	In Favour	In Favour		
China	Imbalanced: "The three articles under consideration were the cornerstone of the convention and should reflect a balance between rights and obligations that was absent from the current proposal [...]. Since the Chairman's proposal was a compromise text and failed to strike a balance between rights and obligations, her delegation could not accept it."	Against	Against		
Czech Republic	Imbalanced: "proposal was unacceptable because the balance between articles 5 and 7 on the one hand and articles 5 and 6 on the other had been lost; that balance had been the basic assumption underlying the negotiations."	Abstain	In Favour		X
Egypt	Balanced: "the Chairman's proposal was balanced and that they were prepared to accept it in order to facilitate a consensus."	Abstain	Abstain		
Ethiopia	Imbalanced: "The new wording, particularly that in paragraph 2 of article 7, where the words "consistent with" had been replaced by "taking into account", upset the balance between articles 5 and 7."	Abstain	Abstain		
Hungary	Balanced: "stressed that the Chairman's text was truly conciliatory and took into account the interests of various groups. He did not agree with those delegations who found it extremely unbalanced. The Chairman should remind participants that it was a compromise text [...]."	In Favour	In Favour	X	X

India	Imbalanced: "Article 5 was therefore totally unacceptable. In the Chairman's proposal, article 7 also departed significantly from the text of the International Law Commission. That article contained many balancing elements which might have been adjusted so as to bear in mind the various points of view."	Abstain	Abstain		
Israel	Imbalanced: "would prefer to see an explicit balance in articles 5 and 7, but was prepared to accept the Chairman's proposal as a compromise solution."	In Favour	Abstain		
Liechtenstein	Imbalanced: "could not accept the wording of article 7, paragraph 2, and deeply regretted that the delicate balance achieved [...] had not been maintained."	In Favour	In Favour		X
Mexico	Balanced: "the Chairman's proposal was balanced and that they were prepared to accept it in order to facilitate a consensus."	In Favour	In Favour		
Portugal	Balanced: "the Chairman's proposal was balanced and that they were prepared to accept it in order to facilitate a consensus."	In Favour	In Favour	X	
Republic of Korea	Balanced: "welcomed the Chairman's proposal, which he viewed as a balanced compromise formula that could not be improved upon."	In Favour	In Favour		X
Romania	Balanced: "the Chairman's proposal was balanced and that they were prepared to accept it in order to facilitate a consensus."	In Favour	In Favour		X
Slovakia	Imbalanced: "the amendment introduced in paragraph 2 of article 7 changed the meaning, the substance and the balance among articles 5, 6 and 7, which were the most important articles of the Convention."	Abstain	In Favour		X
Syrian Arab Republic	Imbalanced: "desirable to strengthen not only article 7, by replacing [...], in order to restore the balance."	In Favour	In Favour	X	
Turkey	Imbalanced: "could not accept the phrase 'taking into account the provisions of articles 5 and 6' in article 7, paragraph 2, because it upset the necessary balance between articles 7 and 5 [...]."	Against	Against		
Vietnam	Balanced: "the Chairman's proposal was balanced and that they were prepared to accept it in order to facilitate a consensus."	In Favour	In Favour	X	

Source: UNGA 1997a, 1997b, 1997c; UNTC 1992, 1997.

Watercourses Convention both at the vote and in the years leading up to its accession (Eckstein 2020; Zhong et al. 2016). Given their similarities, it is likely that these concerns have also hindered, at least in some ways, the accession process of the Water Convention. The Water Convention's innovative mechanisms, such as the Meeting of the Parties and Implementation Committee, however, have provided the much-needed reinforcement to ensure increasing state support.

In many ways, this resolves the discrepancies between state perceptions of these rules and the voting record, as previously discussed. Many states who abstained or voted against the draft were upstream, whereas many of the states who supported it were downstream. Some states, however, claimed that it was balanced or imbalanced but abstained, whereas others claimed it was imbalanced but voted in favour. For example, Egypt and Argentina, both primarily downstream, claimed it was balanced but abstained from the vote. Others, such as Syria and Israel, claimed it was in some way imbalanced but voted in favour. This could be explained by their various positions on the river and a preference for various interpretations of the treaty. For example, in relation to Egypt, such a discrepancy may be explained by its primarily downstream position and longstanding disagreements concerning water allocation with upstream states. Together, this may illustrate that states tend to vote accordingly to what they perceive is in their best interests and do not necessarily strive towards greater legal reciprocity. As illustrated in Chapter 3, however, these positions are, in the long term, untenable and states must recognize the rights of their riparian neighbours.

Interpreting the substantive rules through the lens of reciprocity

Equitable and reasonable use and the duty not to cause significant harm provide the cooperative framework for states to enact limited territorial sovereignty. Unlike the Water Convention which specifically mentions reciprocity as one of its guiding principles of cooperation (1992: art. 2(6), 9(1) & 10), the Watercourses Convention does not explicitly mention reciprocity. However, as a general principle of international law, reciprocity continues to inform state interactions and interpretation of the law, discouraging self-interested interpretation. In line with this and in spite of state perceptions to the contrary, the substantive rules of equitable and reasonable use and the due diligence obligation not to cause significant harm, found in both the Watercourses Convention and Water Convention, are internally and relatively reciprocal.

The Watercourses Convention

The principle of equitable and reasonable utilization

Born out of the concept of limited territorial sovereignty, the principle of equitable and reasonable use acts as a guiding principle of cooperation between riparian neighbours. As such, it establishes a reciprocal obligation of consideration of the interests of other states in order to determine what an equitable and reasonable allocation of a shared water resource is. Found in Article 5 and 6 of the Watercourses Convention, the principle of equitable and reasonable use governs the allocation and apportionment of water in transboundary watercourses. Aiming to protect a state's "equitable share of the uses and benefits of an international watercourse" (McCaffrey 2019: 444), such a rule is based upon the equality of right; however, this does not entail an equal share of water for each watercourse state. Article 5 sets out the rights and duties of the state as well as the goal, to attain "optimal utilization and benefits" (ILC 1994: 97). Framed as an obligation, Article 5(1) requires that states "shall in their respective territories utilize an international watercourse in an equitable and reasonable manner" (1997: art. 5(1)). Furthermore, it establishes the right of watercourse states to an "equitable share, or portion, of the uses and benefits of an international watercourse" (ILC 1994: 97). Meeting this goal requires cooperation, and thus Article 5(2) sets out the right to equitable participation, which includes both the "right to utilize" and the "duty to cooperate." This is followed by Article 6, which provides a non-exhaustive list of factors that are to be used to determine what is considered as "equitable and reasonable."

The principle establishes both the right to an "equitable share, or portion, of the uses and benefits" and the corresponding duty to use this portion in an "equitable and reasonable manner." This does not entail that each state is entitled to an equal share, but instead there exists an "equality of right" which entails an entitlement to the "use and benefit from the watercourse in an equitable manner" (ILC 1994: 98). In determining what is equitable, states must consider the factors listed in Article 6 as a whole, with their weight being determined by their "importance in comparison with that of other relevant factors" (1997: art. 6). Determining what is equitable and reasonable requires an "ongoing comparison" of the conditions and uses in all riparian states (McCaffrey 2019: 462). Thus, all riparian states have the corresponding right to use the waters within their territory, but also the corresponding reciprocal duty to do so in an equitable and reasonable manner, requiring them to "exercise due diligence to avoid depriving co-riparians of their equitable share" (McCaffrey 2019: 463). As such, the principle of equitable and reasonable use does not favour states in any specific geographic position, but provides equal consideration for all in order to achieve an equitable and reasonable balance.

The due diligence obligation not to cause significant harm

Laid out in Article 7, the duty not to cause significant harm establishes the due diligence obligation not to cause significant harm. Article 7(1) introduces the obligation, requiring states to "take all appropriate measures to prevent the causing of significant harm to other watercourse States" (1997: art. 7(1)).

As an obligation of conduct (McCaffrey & Sinjela 1998), it requires states to take appropriate measures to prevent significant harm when possible, and states will be found to be in breach of their obligation when the harm was caused intentionally or due to negligence (ILC 1994). Therefore, states have the right not to be significantly harmed and the corresponding due diligence obligation not to harm their riparian neighbours. The reciprocal nature of the obligation is clear as we move with the flow of the river, since harm is easily understood as flowing downstream. For example, upstream states have an obligation to ensure that upstream pollution does not cause significant harm downstream. The flow of harm from downstream to upstream and the reciprocal rights of upstream states not to be significantly harmed is less obvious.

It is commonly accepted, however, that harm can also flow upstream, ensuring that the duty not to cause significant harm cannot be interpreted to favour either upstream or downstream states. Physical harm, such as the obstruction of fish migration patterns, can affect both upstream and downstream states; however, harm can also be legal (McCaffrey 2019). As Salman explains, "[p]rojects on shared rivers in the downstream riparian states would help those riparians in acquiring, and later claiming, rights to the water abstracted under those projects" (Salman 2010: 352). As such, we could imagine a conflict unfolding in which the earlier developing downstream state makes a legal claim to the right to use those waters, limiting the uses available to the upstream state. Such uses would then be challenged by the upstream state based on equitable and reasonable utilization, while the downstream State would counter this argument with a claim to the duty not to cause significant harm based on their pre-existing uses (Salman 2010). Thus, taking into consideration legal and physical harm completes the reciprocal nature of the obligations within the due diligence obligation not to cause significant harm principle, providing upstream and downstream states with corresponding rights and duties.

The relationship between equitable and reasonable use and the due diligence obligation not to cause significant harm

Over time academics and practitioners have come to an agreement that a careful reading of Articles 5, 6 and 7 of the Watercourses Convention places equitable and reasonable use as the primary rule over the duty not to cause significant harm (McCaffrey 2019: 436; Salman 2007b: 9; Wouters 1999: 294). This conclusion is supported by the *Gabčíkovo-Nagymaros Case*, which referred to equitable and reasonable use but did not mention the due diligence obligation not to cause significant harm.[3] Referred to as "two sides of the same coin" (McCaffrey 2019: 497), together these rules establish a "framework for identifying 'all relevant factors and circumstances' and for evaluating the lawfulness of new or increased uses" (Wouters 2014: 69). This framework "takes into account the needs of all concerned, balancing these needs and taking a decision based on the consideration of the whole"

(Wouters 2014: 69). Article 6 provides a list of factors which need to be taken into consideration when determining an equitable and reasonable use. Although the list of factors is to be taken into consideration as a whole, and each is to be considered and weighted against the others, it includes: "the effects of the use or uses of the watercourse in one watercourse state on other watercourse states," and the "existing and potential uses of the watercourse" (1997: art. 6(d-e)). In this sense, harm is but another factor to be taken into consideration when determining what is equitable and reasonable, and therefore fits into the reciprocal process of consideration established by the principle of equitable and reasonable use. Furthermore, this indicates that some harm, even significant harm, may need to be tolerated in order to establish an equitable and reasonable balance of the shared water resource (McCaffrey 2019). Even though downstream states are likely to have developed earlier, these rules reflect the fact that all riparian states will eventually develop their resources and that some harm must be tolerated (Zeitoun 2015).

The substantive rules of the Water Convention

At the 1989 Conference on Security and Co-operation in Sofia, Bulgaria, it was recommended that the UNECE elaborate upon a framework agreement concerning transboundary waters (Rieu-Clarke 2015: 5–6). Unlike the Watercourses Convention, the Water Convention was adopted and open for signature and ratification after only five meetings of the Working Party on Water Problems over a span of two years (Rieu-Clarke 2015). This quick process was the product of a "shared understanding of the rules and principles related to transboundary waters" (Rieu-Clarke 2015: 12), all made possible because of the political, cultural and economic commonalities of UNECE member states (McCaffrey 2015). Even though it was originally only open to members states of the UNECE, Article 25 and 26 of the Convention was later amended to permit states outside of the UNECE to become a party with the same rights and obligations as UNECE member states (Trombitcaia & Koeppel 2015).

With its vastly different drafting history and regional beginnings, it is not surprising that the Water Convention takes a very different approach than the Watercourses Convention. Whereas the Watercourses Convention places primary attention on issues of allocation, the Water Convention primarily focusses on the reduction of transboundary impact, defined as

> significant adverse effect on the environment resulting from a change in the conditions of transboundary waters caused by a human activity, the physical origin of which is situated wholly or in part within an area under the jurisdiction of a Party, within an area under the jurisdiction of another Party.
>
> (1992: art. 1(2))

Thus, the Water Convention primarily focusses more so on the prevention of pollution and environmental protection (McCaffrey 2015). In spite of this very different structure it is generally accepted as complementary to the Watercourses Convention, establishing a similar structure of rights and duties in regards to the substantive rules, as illustrated by party overlap between the global water conventions.[4]

The due diligence obligation not to cause significant harm

With its primary focus on the reduction of transboundary harm, Article 2(1) of the Water Convention lays out the due diligence obligation not to cause significant harm, stating that "the Parties shall take all appropriate measures to prevent, control and reduce any transboundary impact" (1992: art. 2(1)). These transboundary impacts, according to the aforementioned definition, include both qualitative and quantitative impacts (Tanzi & Kolliopoulos 2015) such as "effects on human health and safety, flora, fauna, soil, air, water, climate, landscape and historical monuments or other physical structures or the interaction among these factors," as well as "cultural heritage or socio-economic conditions resulting from alterations to those factors" (1992: art. 1(2)). Such harms often originate from the waterway; however, they may also include harms originating beyond the waterway, for example, through deforestation, which results in downstream flooding (Tanzi & Kolliopoulos 2015). They are, however, qualified by the term "significant," and therefore, similarly to the Watercourses Convention, states are obligated to exercise due diligence so as to prevent significant transboundary impact to their riparian states. The actions that the state must take in fulfilling their due diligence obligation, however, are heavily influenced by the precautionary principle, the polluter pays principle and sustainable development which inform the actions that form the due diligence obligation (Tanzi & Kolliopoulos 2015). The obligation is made reciprocal by the implied right of a state not to face such significant transboundary impact. Like the definition of harm within the Watercourses Convention, "transboundary impact" within the Water Convention can flow both upstream and downstream given its inclusion of a broad scope of qualitative impacts and its inclusion of "socio-economic conditions" (1992: art. 1(5)).

The principle of equitable and reasonable use

The Water Convention primarily focusses on the prevention of significant transboundary impact; however, it recognizes the principle of equitable and reasonable use, heavily linked to the notion of sustainable development (McIntyre 2015b), as one of its foundational principles. Article 2(2c) states that, in the prevention, control and reduction of transboundary impact, parties shall take appropriate measures so as to "ensure that transboundary waters are used in a reasonable and equitable way, taking into particular account their transboundary character, in the case of activities which cause or are likely to cause transboundary impact" (1992: art. 2(2c)). This includes impacts on "socio-economic conditions," thus recognizing the equality of right of states in their uses of the shared resources (UNECE 2013: para. 101). However, in the implementation of the principle of equitable and reasonable use states are once again guided by basic environmental law principles, most notable for this obligation, sustainable development such that water resources are "managed so that the needs of the present generation are met without compromising the ability of future generations to meet their own needs" (1992: art. 2(5c)). Thus, states have the obligation to manage their waters in an equitable and reasonable manner in terms of transboundary impact of both a qualitative and quantitative nature, with special regard to the principle of sustainable development such that any use that is not sustainable would be inequitable and deemed illegal (UNECE 2013: para. 102). States would also have the corresponding reciprocal right to an equitable and reasonable share of water in terms of both quality and quantity at present and, given the focus on sustainability, also for future generations.

Unlike the Watercourses Convention, the Water Convention does not include a list of factors that are to be taken into consideration to determine what is equitable and reasonable. Noting that the determination of what is equitable and reasonable "depends on the specific circumstances pertaining to the given basin, as well as the social, economic and political features of the States involved," the Guide to the Implementation of the Water Convention points to the interpretation of Article 6(1) of the Watercourses Convention which lists a variety of factors, none of which take priority over the others (UNECE 2013: para. 106–7). While none take priority, the Watercourses Convention gives "special regard" to vital human need (1997: art. 10(2)), and the Guide links this to sustainability, stating that "in weighing up all relevant factors every effort should be made to maximize the resultant benefits to watercourse states equitably, whilst at the same time protecting the long-term sustainability of the resource" (UNECE 2013: para. 108).

The relationship between equitable and reasonable use and the due diligence obligation not to cause significant harm

Given that the Water Convention places heavy emphasis on the mitigation of transboundary impact and leads with the due diligence obligation not to cause significant harm, it may appear that the due diligence obligation not to cause significant harm is placed in a primary role over the rule of equitable and reasonable use. Although the due diligence obligation plays a "prominent role" and represents the "main standard of State conduct" in the Convention, it has been stated that it would "undermine the trust in international water law" to argue that the Water Convention places the due diligence obligation in a prominent position over the principle of equitable and reasonable use (Tanzi & Kolliopoulos 2015: 138–9). The report regarding the connections between the Water Convention and the Watercourses Convention states that the Water Convention presents a "complex substantive normative framework of which both rules, being closely interconnected are [p]art and parcel"

(Tanzi 2015: 28). Thus, there is room for an interpretation in line with the Watercourses Convention in which the principle of equitable and reasonable use is primary. In weighing the necessary factors to determine what is considered to be an equitable and reasonable use, it has been noticed that the Guide provides that "every effort should be made to maximise the resultant benefits to watercourse States equitably, whilst at the same time protecting the long-term sustainability of the resource" (UNECE 2013: para. 108; McIntyre 2015b). The primacy of the principle of equitable and reasonable use is further established given that the Guide confirms that a transboundary use which causes transboundary impact is not necessarily considered to be inequitable, and therefore illegal (UNECE 2013).

The Berlin Rules: an alternative relationship between the substantive rules?

In 1997 the Water Resources Committee of the International Law Association (ILA) set to the task of updating and revising the 1966 Helsinki Rules, which, at the time, were widely regarded as a codification of customary law. After four years of deliberation the Committee released the Berlin Rules, which they regard as incorporating the "experience of nearly four decades since the Helsinki Rules" (ILA 2004: 4), at the 2004 Berlin Conference. The report indicates that the intention of the committee was to

> provide a clear, cogent and coherent statement of the customary international law that applies to waters of international drainage basins, and to the extent that customary international law applies to waters entirely within a state, to all waters as well. These Rules also undertake the progressive development of the law needed to cope with emerging problems of international or global water management for the twenty-first century.
>
> (ILA 2004: 3)

The resulting rules, which take into consideration developments in environmental, humanitarian and human rights law, are comprised of 73 articles divided into 14 chapters (Salman 2007a). Even though the report indicates that all in attendance at the previous meeting had voted to present the Berlin Rules to the ILA,[5] four members of the committee strongly disagreed with the Report and submitted a Dissenting Opinion to the Committee. Their dissenting opinion took issue with the scope of the rules, which covers both international and national waters, its use of the term "shall," and, most importantly for this chapter, its treatment of the principle of equitable utilization (Bogdanovic et al. 2004).

Although both the Watercourses Convention and Water Convention place the principle of equitable and reasonable use in a primary role over the due diligence obligation not to cause significant harm, the relationship between the two principles in the Berlin Rules is unclear. Found in Article 12, states "shall in their respective territories manage the waters of an international drainage basin in an equitable and reasonable manner having due regard for the obligation not to cause significant harm to other basin states" (ILA 2004: art. 12). The term "manage" includes the "development, use, protection, allocation, regulation and control of waters" (ILA 2004: art. 3(14)). According to the Committee, such a formulation recognizes that "with the right to share come obligations that can only be fulfilled by acting in an equitable and reasonable manner, having due regard to the obligation not to cause significant harm" (ILA 2004: art. 20). Such wording of the principle of equitable and reasonable use places emphasis on the obligation to manage, not the right to an equitable and reasonable share (Salman 2007a). Therefore, when analysed on its own Article 12 provides states with a duty to manage their water resources in an equitable and reasonable manner, but does not explicitly include the corresponding right to utilize an equitable and reasonable share of those waters.

This corresponding right to an equitable and reasonable share of the waters comes out in Article 16, which deals with significant transboundary harm. Whereas mention of "harm" or "damage" is spread throughout the Rules,[6] transboundary harm is dealt with in Article 16 – Avoidance of Transboundary Harm, which provides that states

> in managing the waters of an international drainage basin, shall refrain from and prevent acts or omissions within their territory that cause significant harm to another basin State having due regard for the right of each basin state to make equitable and reasonable use of the waters.
>
> (ILA 2004: art. 16)

Under this view, states have the duty not to cause significant harm to other basin states; however, the corresponding right not to be significantly harmed appears to come from the states right to an equitable and reasonable use (ILA 2004: art. 12). Thus, it appears that each principle is subjected to each other, and that they are, on some level, equal (Salman 2007a). It could also be concluded, however, that the due diligence obligation not to cause significant harm is primary over the principle of equitable and reasonable use (Bogdanovic et al. 2004). Regardless of which interpretation is preferred, the Berlin Rules appear to create confusion in an area where, as earlier illustrated, states already exhibit confusion.

China's transboundary water treaty practice: the substantive rules

The reciprocal character of limited territorial sovereignty is one of the foundations of China's approach to its transboundary waters, consistent with China's approach to international law generally. A closer look at China's treaty practice indicates that it highly values the reciprocal nature of the substantive rules in its transboundary water agreements; however, it is often couched in vague terms and corresponds to the levels of cooperation across its transboundary waters, found more often in the Northeast and Northwest. Many of China's transboundary treaties recognize the principle of equitable and reasonable use, but the principle is often accompanied by language which shows a preference for its reciprocal nature such as, among others, "fairness," "mutual benefit," and "coexistence." The preamble of the 2008 China–Russia Agreement on the Rational Utilization and Protection of Transboundary Waters places these guiding principles alongside equitable and reasonable utilization, basing cooperation on "peaceful co-existence, mutual understanding, equitable and reasonable utilization and protection" (Vinogradov & Wouters 2013: 36). The 2001 China–Russia Treaty of Good-Neighbourliness and Friendly Cooperation, Article 19, includes the principle of equitable and reasonable use, placing it alongside the concept of fairness, stating that the "contracting parties shall carry out cooperation in [...] the fair and rational use of water resources along the border areas" (2001: art. 19). The 1994 China–Mongolia Agreement on the Protection and Utilization of Transboundary Waters states that the parties will conduct cooperation in various fields "for the purpose of protection and equitable and rational use of transboundary waters [...]," going on to state that "any development and utilization of transboundary waters should follow the principle of fairness and equability without impeding any reasonable use of transboundary waters" (1994: art. 2 & 4). The 2001 China–Kazakhstan Agreement calls for states to "adhere to the principles of equity and rationality" (2001: art. 2), going on to elaborate upon its reciprocal structure, stating that "no Party shall limit the other Party in the rational use and protection of the water resources of transboundary rivers" (China–Kazakhstan 2001: art. 4). Furthermore, the 2013 China–Kazakhstan Joint Declaration on Further Deepening Comprehensive Strategic Partnership states that "the two sides will use transboundary water resources fairly and reasonably" (2013: sect. 3, para. 3). In 2005, China and Bangladesh released a Joint Communiqué indicating that they would increase cooperation, "keeping in mind the principles of equality and fairness" (2005: para. 11). Although China recognizes the principle of equitable and reasonable use it is often presented in vague terms. Unlike the Watercourses Convention, which provides a list of factors that are to be taken into consideration when determining what is to be considered an equitable and reasonable use in Article 6, it is unclear from China's treaties how we are to determine whether a use is "fair," "rational" or "equitable." The 2008 China–Russia Agreement, however, indicates that it should take into consideration "economic, social and demographic factors" (Vinogradov & Wouters 2013: 36). While China accepts the principle of equitable and reasonable use as the "cornerstone" of the law of transboundary waters, it is unclear if equitable and reasonable use enjoys primacy over the duty not to cause significant harm as it does in the Watercourses Convention and Water Convention.

China affirms the duty not to cause significant harm and its due diligence nature (Wouters & Chen 2013) as exemplified in treaties with Kazakhstan; however, its treaties often focus on harms that flow downstream potentially limiting reciprocal application and possibly being overly burdensome for upstream China. The 2001 China–Kazakhstan Agreement, for example, limits harm stating that "Parties shall undertake appropriate measures and shall make efforts to prevent or mitigate serious harm caused to a State Party as a result of flooding disasters and man-made accidents" (2001: art. 3). Agreements with Mongolia and Russia, however, are more in line with a reciprocal approach, leaving interpretation open to various forms of harm that can flow downstream as well as upstream. For example, the 1994 China–Mongolia Agreement indicates that parties should "develop and utilize transboundary waters in a way that should not be detrimental to the other side" (1994: art. 4). In 2005, a chemical spill in Northeastern China entered the Songhua and Heilong rivers, flowing into Russian territory. In recognition of its obligation not to cause significant harm, China notified Russia and also entered into a more active phase of cooperation with its neighbour, resulting in the 2006 Agreement on the Management of the China–Russia Border, as well as the 2008 China–Russia Agreement which states that parties should "take all necessary measures to prevent significant harm caused by transboundary impact" (Vinogradov & Wouters 2013: 37).

Whereas the substantive rules appear in agreements in the Northeast and Northwest, beyond the 2005 Bangladesh–China Joint Communiqué there is little mention of these principles in treaties and related documents on the Southwest. The newly established Lancang-Mekong Cooperation (LMC) Mechanism does not specifically mention rules or principles regarding the allocation of water resources or the prevention of harm; however, the participating states aim to "enhance cooperation [...] in sustainable water resources management and utilization" (LMC 2016: para. 10). Even without specific rules or principles regarding water allocation, the LMC states are bound by the reciprocal process laid out in these rules given their status as customary international law. Furthermore, the lower riparians are bound by these rules as they are present within the 1995 Mekong River Agreement (MRC 1995).

The influence of common interests on the substantive rules and China's practice

Although reciprocity has played a large role in the establishment and maintenance of the international legal system, its role in certain areas of international law is changing. In certain emerging areas the legal principle of reciprocity "appears to do more harm than good," where negative reciprocation could act as justification for the legalization of torture, production of nuclear weapons and an "inevitable race to the bottom" all because other fellow states did so (Paulus 2011: 114). The changing influence of reciprocity is exemplified in various new and emerging areas of international law which reflect common interests, such as human rights and environmental protection. These areas of "common interest" cannot function relying solely upon reciprocal conceptions of international law, as the duties in these areas are, in many ways, unilateral (Brunée 1989: 796). While reciprocity's role may be limited, treaties in these areas still follow a reciprocal structure of rights and duties, but differ in the sense that they do not involve any material benefits (Simma 2008). These developments are evidenced in the law of international watercourses through the establishment of the human right to water as well as the increasing focus on environmental protection, both of which could be viewed as non-reciprocating provisions. Such provisions have "tempered, at least in theory" (Simma 1989: 844) bilateralist obligations, exemplified by the influence such community interests have on the substantive rules through the human right to water and the notion of sustainability. As the substantive rules, particularly equitable and reasonable use, establish standards and the operational approach to achieve them (Wouters & Rieu-Clarke 2001), these community interests will impact that standard.

The human right to water in a transboundary context

The human right to water, as a derived right from the right to health and the right to an adequate standard of living, has been present in a series of rights documents over the past few decades. It has, however, more recently come into form in 2010 when the Human Rights Committee released General Comment No 15 (UNCESCR 2002), followed by its subsequent adoption by the UNGA through Resolution 64/292 (UNGA 2010), and the Human Rights Council Resolution 15/9 (UNHRC 2010). As an authoritative interpretation of the International Covenant on Economic, Social and Cultural Rights (ICCPR 1976), General Comment No. 15 sets out the content of the right as entitling "everyone to sufficient, safe, acceptable, physically accessible and affordable water for personal and domestic uses" (UNCESCR 2002: para. 2) The right holder has both freedoms and entitlements, with states having the "core obligation" to "ensure access to the minimum essential amount of water, that is sufficient and safe for personal and domestic uses to prevent disease," among others (UNCESCR 2002: para. 10 & 37(a–i)). In the pursuit of this right, states have obligations to respect, protect and fulfil the basic water needs of their citizens (UNCESCR 2002).

Although at a practical level, it may be true that the role of reciprocity is limited in human rights law given the state-citizen nature of the rights and duties that are created, reciprocity still plays a role. It is also the case that if one state violates provisions of a human rights treaty, other states are not permitted to do the same in retaliation (Posner 2012: 161). At a legal level, however, human rights treaties are reciprocal in the sense that each party has an interest in the other party "contributing to the realization of legal regimes in the community interest" (Simma 2008: para. 6). This was reflected in General Comment No. 31 of the Human Rights Committee, which states that "every State Party has a legal interest in the performance of every other State Party of its obligations" (UNHRC 2004: para. 2). This contractual aspect of such treaties ensures that state parties have an obligation owed to every other party to comply with the treaty (Klein 2011; UNHRC 2004).

As a human right, the right to water would have a similar non-reciprocal structure as other human rights as it is primarily a state who must fulfil its obligations towards its citizens. In transboundary situations, however, the implementation of the human right to water may have international implications as states may need to assist their fellow riparian states in meeting the basic water needs of their citizens (Leb 2012). Present in both the global water conventions, the human right to water tempers the reciprocal aspects of the substantive rules, providing a basic standard that must be met regardless of the reciprocal allocation of shared waters.

Article 10 of the Watercourses Convention provides that no use shall have "inherent priority" over others; however, it goes on to state that any conflict between uses shall be dealt with by referring to the reciprocal process of the substantive rules in Article 5–7, with "special regard being given to the requirements of vital human needs" (1997: art. 10(2)). Such vital human needs involve "providing sufficient water to sustain human life, including both drinking water and water required for the production of food in order to prevent starvation" (ILC 1994: 110). As such, when undertaking the reciprocal process found within the interplay of the substantive rules, uses and harms that affect the quantity and quality of water for individuals in other states must be taken into consideration (Leb 2012; McCaffrey 2017), such that a use that does not align with vital human needs would be "inherently inequitable and unreasonable" (Tanzi & Arcari 2001: 141; ILC 1994).

Given its complementary character, as earlier illustrated, the substantive rules of the Water Convention could also be interpreted to protect vital human needs. For example, when referring to the principle of equitable and reasonable use within the Water Convention, the Guide refers to "vital human need" within the Watercourses Convention. It then goes on to say that no agreeement could preclude inequitable uses, such as "a use that would irreversibly affect the environment to the extent of impairing present or future vital human needs of the people living along the basin, or beyond" (UNECE 2013: 25). Where it differs, however, is in the series of procedural aspects required to respect, protect and fulfil access to water found within the 1999 Protocol on Water and Health to the Water Convention. Notwithstanding that the human right to water is not mentioned in the Protocol (Leb 2012; McIntyre 2015c; Tanzi 2010) and that the Protocol was completed before the aforementioned documents concerning the right, it can be argued that the Protocol acts as a tool to implement the right to access to water (Tanzi 2010). Completed to promote "the protection of human health and well-being" at the national and international level (UNECE 1999: art. 1), parties to the Protocol shall "take all appropriate measures" so as to ensure "adequate supplies of wholesome drinking water" (UNECE 1999: art. 6).

Although adopted well before the release of General Comment No. 15, multiple scholars have pointed out that the Protocol closely follows the requirements of the General Comment (Leb 2012; McIntyre 2015c; Tanzi 2010). In terms of transboundary waters, the Protocol lays out a series of cooperative measures that state parties should take so as to promote access and protection of human health. Based upon the duty to cooperate found in Article 11, these measures include the exchange of information, development of common targets and indicators, establishment of joint monitoring and surveillance, assisting each other in cases of outbreaks and incidents, among others (UNECE 1999: art. 12). Most importantly, however, Article 13 states that parties "shall cooperate and, as appropriate, assist each other to prevent, control and reduce transboundary effects of water-related disease" (UNECE 1999). Similar to Article 11, states also follow a series of procedural rules, and alter their agreements on the "basis of equality and reciprocity" so as to "eliminate any contradictions with the basic principles" of the Protocol (UNECE 1999: art. 13(c)).

Environmental protection and sustainability

Given that cooperation concerning the environment is more like a "joint venture" than a reciprocal exchange, it does not easily lend itself to reciprocity (Conca 2001: 234). When environmental impacts on the system are viewed as a whole; however, there are many opportunities for reciprocal exchange and areas of cooperation can emerge where effective exchange can take place (Conca 2001). Similar to provisions of human rights treaties, treaty provisions concerning the environment often involve unilateral action within a state's sovereign territory, but given the interconnected nature of our planet and the ecosystems within, opportunities for exchange emerge. Such exchange, however, often takes place in a more future-oriented manner, where reciprocal exchange provides future benefits for joint action today (Conca 2001). The substantive rules, however, are tempered by community interest norms, particularly sustainable development which entails that "any development policy must equitably meet developmental and environmental needs of both present and future generations" (Spijkers et al. 2016: 208). This notion of sustainable development thus not only takes into consideration harmful environmental impact, but the need to consider "vital human need," as discussed above, at present and for future generations (McIntyre 2007).

The Watercourses Convention provides multiple obligations regarding environmental protection, many of which are unilateral. Article 20 indicates that states "shall, individually and, where appropriate, jointly, protect and preserve the ecosystems of international watercourses." In controlling pollution, states shall "individually and, where appropriate, jointly, prevent, reduce and control" pollution "that may cause significant harm to other watercourses States or to their environment" (1997: art. 21(2)). States are also obliged to prevent the introduction of alien species, protect the marine environment, conduct consultations in regards to management, cooperate concerning the regulation of flow, as well as maintain, protect and consult regarding installations or facilities (1997: art. 22–26).

Beyond these provisions requiring unilateral action within their own territory, considerations of sustainability intersect with the substantive rules in both the Watercourses Convention and Water Convention. This is most notable through the notion of sustainable development, as these rules operationalize this notion (McIntyre 2017). Given that a focus on sustainability and environmental protection permeates the Water Convention, the impact of this notion on that Convention has already been discussed above. Sustainability, however, also impacts the substantive rules in the Watercourses Convention. In order to determine what is equitable and reasonable states must take a list of factors into consideration. This is evident through the inclusion of "climatic, ecological and other factors of a natural character," the "effects of the use or uses of the watercourses [...]," "conservation" and "protection," and the special consideration given to "vital human need" which provides a focus on present and future generations (1997: art. 6(1a, d & f) & 10). As such, uses that are not sustainable may be deemed harmful, inequitable and therefore illegal, providing a base standard for the substantive rules.

China's transboundary water treaty practice: the influence of common interests

China's legal practice is also influenced by norms in the community interest, exemplified by its support for the human right to water and increasing environmentalization founded on the notion of sustainable development in China's transboundary water treaties. China supported the human right to water at its adoption by the UNGA through Resolution 64/292. While the content of the human right to water has yet to be clearly defined in a transboundary context, it may entail a limited obligation for water-rich states to provide water-scarce neighbours with enough water so as to fulfil the basic needs of their people (Leb 2012). China's strong stance on state sovereignty entails that it prefers not to interfere in the affairs of other states; however, it does appear to assist them when needed through coordinated efforts. Although it's unclear if these cases are directly related to upholding the human right to water, they illustrate that China understands that, in certain situations, its obligations may entail the provision of water to its neighbours. In 2014 after experiencing drought, Kazakhstan made a request to China for assistance, and China responded by releasing waters from Sandaohezi Station on the Ili River for a period of ten days (Xie & Jia 2018). Even though no agreement concerning allocation exists between China and its Lancang-Mekong riparians, in 2013 China released waters from upstream dams on the Lancang-Mekong to alleviate downstream drought (Tian & Liu 2016). It did so again at the request of Vietnam in 2016, when China doubled its release of water from upstream dams to alleviate severe drought downstream. A spokesperson from the Chinese Ministry of Foreign Affairs is quoted as saying that "people living along the Lancang-Mekong River are nourished by the same river. It goes without saying that friends should help each other when help is needed" (Tiezzi 2016). When the region was again experiencing severe drought in late 2019, China released water from its upstream dams to alleviate downstream drought in early 2020 (The Nation 2020; Embassy to Thailand 2020). As discussed in Chapter 2, it should be noted that hydropower across the region, but particularly those on the upper reaches of the Lancang-Mekong have come under significant criticism as the potential source of these recurring droughts, a claim finding some support in recent studies (for example, Räsänen et al. 2017; MRC 2019). China, however, has stated that these dams provide flood and drought relief (Embassy to Thailand 2019), pointing to Mekong River Commission (MRC) studies indicating that, although these dams may impact fish migration and sediment flows, that these dams have not reduced flows during the dry season (MRC 2017). This situation continues to evolve, and greater collaboration between China and its Lancang-Mekong riparians appears to be forthcoming.

A select few of China's transboundary water treaties offer a series of measures to protect the transboundary environment. In, for example, the 2001 China–Russia Treaty, Article 19 indicates that parties "shall carry out cooperation in the protection and improvement of the environment, prevention of cross-border pollution [...]." Furthermore, the 1994 China–Mongolia Agreement, Article 6 states that parties "shall take measures to prevent, mitigate and eliminate the possible damages to the quality, resources and natural dynamics of the transboundary waters and aquatic animals and plants caused by natural or human factors." The common interest aspects of the substantive rules are also found within China's transboundary treaties (Spijkers et al. 2016). For example, the 2011 China–Kazakhstan Agreement on the Protection of Water Quality of Transboundary Rivers states that, in regards to pollution prevention, "both parties recognize their responsibilities towards contemporary and future generations" (Spijkers et al. 2016: 212). Furthermore, the 1994 Memorandum of Understanding on Environmental Principles Governing the Tumen River Economic Development Area and Northeast Asia has as its goal "to attain environmentally sound and sustainable development of Northeast Asia and the Tumen River Economic Development Area" (1994: objectives). The parties commit themselves to "conduct[ing] all development activities in the Region in a manner that does not damage the environment of any Contracting Party," agreeing to a series of protection measures to do so (Tumen 1994: art. 1(4)).

Institutionalizing reciprocity through river basin organizations and benefit-sharing

The reciprocal nature of the substantive rules of the law of international watercourses are clear in basins with two riparians with clearly assigned rights and duties, but as the number of riparians increases so too does the complexity of obligations. Although bilateral obligations can greatly benefit from some form of institutionalized management, the complexity of rights and obligations in multilateral river basins lends itself more clearly to institutionalization through river basin organizations (RBOs), commissions or some form of joint body. Furthermore, given the complexity of the rights and obligations involved, a series of procedural rules including prior notification, consultation and data sharing are necessary in order to support the ongoing process to determine what is equitable and reasonable, as well as where and when harm or transboundary impact has occurred, among other things. While neither general international law nor the Watercourses Convention oblige states to form such basin management organizations (Earle & Wouters 2015), McCaffrey notes that such organizations are "almost indispensable if anything approaching optimum utilization and protection of the system of water is to be attained" (McCaffrey 1990: 44, para. 7). The Water Convention, however, obligates states to establish joint bodies in any agreements concerning their transboundary waters (1992: art. 9(2)).

Whether or not states are obligated to form such joint bodies, RBOs act as a natural focal point for states to communicate and reciprocate with their riparian neighbours, providing "concrete returns for relinquishing some of their sovereignty" (Earle & Wouters 2015: 102). RBOs can take on multiple forms and responsibilities (Schmeier 2013), acting as a potential staging ground for furthering the reciprocal balance between riparian states. Given the intricacies of hydrological systems and the realities of basin development,[7] it may be extremely difficult to establish an equitable and reasonable balance that satisfies the interests of all states. In these instances, some states may believe that they are contributing or are entitled to more than their riparian neighbour. Such imbalances, however, can be softened via cooperation between states in the form of benefit-sharing agreements. Said to have first originated as part of the Columbia River Treaty (McKenzie 2013; Paisley 2002), benefit-sharing can be defined as "any action designed to change the allocation of costs and benefits associated with cooperation" (Sadoff & Grey 2005: 422). In other words, benefit-sharing aims to distribute benefits to the river, from the river, because of the river and beyond the river (Sadoff & Grey 2005), as well as the costs of such cooperation. Sometimes referred to as a general principle of the law of international watercourses and environmental law (Tarlock & Wouters 2007), a legal framework for benefit-sharing would allow states to take a balanced approach even in instances where the equivalence of costs and benefits of their rights and duties may not allow them to do so. Furthermore, it permits states to "optimize benefits and allocate costs," since such a framework would provide "for the equitable sharing of those benefits and costs" (McIntyre 2015a: 51). Although these programmes can bring further balance, they are not without cost, and benefit-sharing frameworks may not necessarily assist with poverty alleviation or take environmental concerns into consideration (Tarlock & Wouters 2007). This is not always the case, however, as benefits do not necessarily need to be project-related, and instead can include payment for ecological benefits, such as ecological stewardship of headwaters (Sadoff & Grey 2005).

China's transboundary water treaty practice: institutionalization and benefit-sharing

Given China's upstream location, and its economic and military dominance, some argue that China acts as a hydro-hegemon, and that it has very little incentive to cooperate with its riparian neighbours (Lowi 1995). China appears, however, to be slowly moving towards cooperation, further supported by ever-increasing interconnectivity with its riparian neighbours (Chen et al. 2013; Su 2014; Wouters & Chen 2013), placing it in a position where the establishment of RBOs and benefit-sharing are of particular importance. China is a member of multiple joint bodies concerning its transboundary waters with India, Kazakhstan, Mongolia and Russia, including the China–India Expert Level Mechanism on Transborder Rivers (China–India 2006), Sino-Kazakh Commission on the use and Protection of Transboundary Rivers, the Sino-Kazakh Commission on Cooperation in the Field of Environmental Protection, the Sino-Mongolian Joint Commission on Transboundary Waters and the Sino-Russian Joint Commission on the Reasonable Utilization and Protection of Transboundary Waters (Chen et al. 2013). China is not a member of the MRC but is a "dialogue partner," and has an agreement with the MRC to provide hydrological data (Chen et al. 2013). Although the LMC has a broad scope, it too acts as a body for the discussion of transboundary water issues between China and the Mekong states, regularly hosting meetings regarding transboundary water resources (Devlaeminck 2020).

Furthermore, providing the impetus for cooperation with its southern neighbours is increasing interconnectivity, through which these states are able to share the benefits of the Mekong. For example, as part of the Greater Mekong Subregion programme through the Asian Development Bank, an interconnected power grid is being established throughout the region, and economic and political exchange is increasing. Due to its growing need for energy, China imports large amounts of hydropower from its downstream neighbours, primarily Laos and Myanmar. These energy imports require a peaceful and healthy relationship between riparians, acting as a catalyst for greater Chinese cooperation (Lee 2015; Ptak & Hommel 2016). Such interconnectivity arguably counteracts aspects of China's hydro-hegemony, since areas of its own development is now dependent on the success of its neighbours, while also revealing common agendas in non-water issues, allowing riparian states to resolve conflicts concerning water (Lee 2015: 149).

Conclusion

At the 20th Meeting of the 6th Committee for the drafting of the Watercourses Convention the delegate for Switzerland stated that

> the draft articles imposed excessive obligations on upstream states that were planning measures […] if such trends persisted, upstream states,

> which should be partners and not adversaries of downstream states, would have no further interest in becoming parties to the convention. Only a balanced and moderate approach could give the convention some semblance of universality.
>
> (UNGA 1996d: 8)

China, an upstream state on almost all of its transboundary waters, at first supported the draft of the Watercourses Convention, but as the conversation progressed, it too argued that the Draft Articles were imbalanced, ultimately voting against the Convention. Such perceived imbalances are based upon misperceptions of the substantive rules of the law of international watercourses, one that favours one position over another; equitable and reasonable use which purportedly favours upstream states, and the duty not to cause significant harm, which purportedly favours downstream states. Reciprocity as a legal principle, however, informs their interpretation in such a way as not to favour states in either position.

While states may perceive equitable and reasonable use as protecting the interests of upstream states, as evident in both the Watercourses Convention and the Water Convention, the substantive rules of the law of international watercourses actually provide a process through which the interests of all riparians must be taken into consideration. Furthermore, even though states may perceive the duty not to cause significant harm as protecting the interests of downstream states, harm actually flows both ways and thus all states are equally susceptible, although to different kinds of harm. Given the primacy of the principle of equitable and reasonable use, some harm may even need to be tolerated by certain states in order to establish an equitable and reasonable balance of uses. China has faced significant criticism concerning the way it manages its transboundary water relations; however, its approach does not appear to be far off from the global water conventions. China's practice appears to follow a reciprocal structure, as evidenced through its treaty practice. Where they differ, however, is in the level of detail. Whereas the substantive rules have a reciprocal structure of rights and duties, the Watercourses Convention and Water Convention contain obligations in the community interest which do not follow such a structure. Community interests, however, are interacting with and influencing the reciprocal structure, most notably in the law of international watercourses through the emergence of the human right to water and the notion of sustainability. Both of which guide the implementation of the substantive rules.

An analysis of these principles through the lens of reciprocity, however, provides much-needed depth and clarity concerning the substantive rules of the law of international watercourses, highlighting processes and areas of exchange which may serve to enhance opportunities for cooperation. As these opportunities are utilized and these obligations become more complicated, it becomes desirable, if not necessary, to conduct such cooperation through some form of RBO or joint commission. Although the equitable and reasonable balance struck by these principles may not be perfect given the hydrological conditions of the basin, the emerging practice of benefit-sharing is one way in which states can bring further balance, with China and its riparians acting as an example.

Acknowledgements

A version of this chapter first appeared as an article in the journal *Water Policy*. For the original article, see Devlaeminck, D. (2018). Revisiting the Substantive Rules of the Law of International Watercourses: An Analysis Through the Lens of Reciprocity and the Interests of China. *Water Policy*, *20*(2), 323–35. It has been reproduced with permission from the copyright holders, IWA Publishing. Sections of this chapter also appeared in the *Chinese Journal of Environmental Law*. For the original article, see Devlaeminck, D. J. (2018). The Legal Principle of Reciprocity and China's Water Treaty Practice. *Chinese Journal of Environmental Law, 2*(2), 195–222.

Notes

1 For Franck, optimal fairness discourse requires: 1) moderate scarcity where actors can expect a reasonable share, but not the entirety of a resource and 2) a community based on "a common, conscious system of reciprocity between its constituents" which leads to a fairness dialogue. Such moderate scarcity greatly reflects the status of water resources in the world, and is reflected in the customary rules of international water law, primarily limited territorial sovereignty and equitable and reasonable use (Franck 1995: 10). For an application of Franck's concept of fairness as it relates to the law of international watercourses (see Yihdego & Rieu-Clarke 2016).

2 In his third report on State Responsibility, James Crawford lists various fields that may be considered "collective interests," including, but not limited to: human rights, human development, world heritage and environmental protection. The Commentary to the Articles on State Responsibility builds upon this list, by adding obligations which concern the "security of a region (e.g. a regional nuclear-free zone treaty or a regional system for the protection of human rights)" (Crawford 2000: 30; ARSIWA 2001: 126).

3 It should be noted, however, that it is likely that the duty not to cause significant harm was not mentioned because harm was not found to have occurred in that case (Wouters 1999).

4 At the time of writing, 17 of the 44 Water Convention parties are also party to the Watercourses Convention (UNTC 1992; 1997).

5 The 4th Report indicates that all those in "attendance" at the previous meeting were in favour of presenting the Rules to the ILA. However, one member who could not attend indicated by email that they were opposed. Furthermore, it indicates that the Rules "represent the view of the majority of the Committee." It also states, however, that it is likely that "few members individually agree with each and every provision of the Rules" (ILA 2004: 3).

6 Multiple articles of the Berlin Rules mention "damage" or "harm" of some sort. See: Article 8 – Minimization of Environmental Harm, Article 15(2) – Using Allocated Water in Other Basin States; Article 16 – Avoidance of Transboundary Harm, Article 23 – The Precautionary Approach, Article 27 – Pollution, Article 30 – Participation in Impact Assessment in Another State, Article 31(d) – The Impact

Assessment Process, Article 32 – Response to Extreme Conditions, Article 34 – Floods, Article 42 – Transboundary Aquifers, Article 52 – Ecological Targets, Article 54 – Occupied Territories, Article 64 – Establishing Basin Wide or Other Joint Management Arrangements, Article 69 – Access to Courts or Administrative Authorities, Article 70 – Remedies for Damage to Persons, and Article 71 – Remedies for Persons in Other States (ILA 2004).

7 Although the substantive rules do not give priority to prior uses, in practice these prior uses will have some priority. For example, in *Province of La Pampa v. Province of Mendoza* (1987) the Supreme Court of Argentina granted the use of the whole of the waters of the Atuel River to the Province of Mendoza, a decision which was made after taking into consideration multiple factors, weighing Mendoza's prior agricultural, domestic and economic uses against La Pampa's need (Fuentes 1997).

References

ARSIWA (2001). Draft Articles on Responsibility of States for Internationally Wrongful Acts with Commentaries. Retrieved from https://legal.un.org/ilc/texts/instruments/english/commentaries/9_6_2001.pdf

Bangladesh–China (2005). Joint Communiqué between the Government of the People's Republic of China and the Government of the People's Republic of Bangladesh (adopted April 8, 2005).

Bodansky, D. (2010). *The Art and Craft of International Environmental Law*. Cambridge/London: Harvard University Press.

Bogdanovic, S., Bourne, C., Burchi, S. & Wouters, P. (2004). Berlin Conference – Dissenting Opinion. Retrieved from www.internationalwaterlaw.org/documents/intldocs/ILA/ILABerlinRulesDissent2004.pdf

Brunée, J. (1989). "Common Interest" – Echoes from an Empty Shell? Some Thoughts on Common Interest and International Environmental Law. *ZaoRV*, *49*(3–4), 791–808.

Byers, M. (2004). *Custom, Power and the Power of Rules: International Relations and Customary Law*. Cambridge: Cambridge University Press.

Chen, H., Rieu-Clarke, A. & Wouters, P. (2013). Exploring China's Transboundary Water Treaty Practice Through the Prism of the UN Watercourses Convention. *Water International*, *38*(2), 217–30.

China–Kazakhstan (2001). Agreement on Cooperation in the Use and Protection of Transboundary Rivers (signed February 22, 2001).

China–Kazakhstan (2013). Joint Declaration on Further Deepening Comprehensive Strategic Partnership (signed September 7, 2013).

China–India (2006). Joint Declaration by the Republic of India and the People's Republic of China (adopted November 21, 2006).

China–Mongolia (1994). Agreement on the Protection and Utilization of Transboundary Waters (signed April 29, 1993).

China–Russia (2001). Treaty of Good-Neighbourliness and Friendly Cooperation (signed July 16, 2001).

Conca, K. (2001). Environmental Cooperation and International Peace. In P. F. Diehl & N. P. Gleditsch (Eds.), *Environmental Conflict* (pp. 225–51). Boulder, Colorado: Westview.

Crawford, J. (2000). Third Report on State Responsibility (A/CN.4/507). Retrieved from http://legal.un.org/docs/?path=../ilc/documentation=/english/a_cn4_507.pdf&lang=EFSX

Dellapenna, J., Rieu-Clarke, A. & Loures, F. R. (2013). Possible Reasons Slowing Down the Ratification Process In F. R. Loures & A. Rieu-Clarke (Eds.), *The UN Watercourses Convention in Force: Strengthening international law for transboundary water management* (pp. 20–7). New York: Earthscan.

Devlaeminck, D. J. (2020). Timeline of the Lancang-Mekong Cooperation (LMC) Mechanism. *Academia.edu*. Retrieved from https://chongqing.academia.edu/David Devlaeminck

Earle, A. & Wouters, P. (2015). Implementing Transboundary Water Cooperation Through Effective Institutional Mechanisms: Exploring the Legal and Institutional Design Dimensions of Selected African Joint Water Institutions – Creating Lessons for Global Problems?. *Journal of Water Law, 24*, 100–14.

Eckstein, G. (2020). The Status of the UN Watercourses Convention: Does it still hold water? *International Journal of Water Resources Development, 36*(2–3), 429–61.

Embassy to Thailand (2019). Chinese Embassy Spokesperson's Remarks on Mekong-related Media Report Targeting China. *Embassy of the People's Republic of China in the Kingdom of Thailand* – June 5. Retrieved from www.chinaembassy.or.th/eng/sgxw/t1678896.htm

Embassy to Thailand (2020). China Increases Water Outflow of Lancang River to Downstream Areas. *Embassy of the People's Republic of China in the Kingdom of Thailand* – January 24. Retrieved from www.chinaembassy.or.th/eng/sgxw/t1736056.htm

Fard, S. N. (2016). *Reciprocity in International Law: Its Impact and Function*. Abingdon/New York: Routledge.

Fitzmaurice, G. G. (1958). Third Report on the Law of Treaties (A/CN.4/115 and Corr. 1). *Yearbook of the International Law Commission, 2*, 21–46.

Franck, T. (1995). *Fairness in International Law and Institutions*. Oxford: Oxford University Press.

Fry, J. D. & Chong, A. (2016). International Water Law and China's Management of Its International Rivers. *Boston College International and Comparative Law Review, 39*(2), 227–66.

Fuentes, X. (1997). The Criteria for the Equitable Utilization of International Rivers, *British Yearbook of International Law, 67*(1), 337–412.

ICCPR (1976). International Covenant on Civil and Political Rights (adopted December 16, 1966; entered into force March 23, 1976).

ICJ (1969). North Sea Continental Shelf Case (Federal Republic of Germany v. Denmark/Federal Republic of Germany v. Netherlands) – Judgement, (International Court of Justice, February 20, 1969).

ILA (1966). The Helsinki Rules on the Uses of the Waters of International Rivers (adopted August 1966).

ILA (2004). 4th Report, Berlin Conference (adopted August 2004).

ILC (1994). The Law of Non-Navigational Uses of International Watercourses: Draft Articles and Commentaries Thereto Adopted by the Drafting Committee on Second Reading (A/CN.4/L.493). *Yearbook of the International Law Commission, II*(2), 89–135.

Klein, E. (2011). Denunciation of Human Rights Treaties and the Principle of Reciprocity. In R. G. Ulrich Fastenrath, Daniel-Erasmus Khan, Andreas Paulus, Sabine von Schorlemer & Christoph Vedder (Eds.), *From Bilateralism to Community Interest: Essays in Honour of Bruno Simma* (pp. 478–87). Oxford: Oxford University Press.

Leb, C. (2012). The Right to Water in a Transboundary Context: Emergence of Seminal Trends. *Water International, 37*(6), 640–53.

Leb, C. (2013). *Cooperation in the Law of Transboundary Water Resources.* Cambridge: Cambridge University Press.

Leb, C. (2014). One Step at a Time: International Law and the Duty to Cooperate in the Management of Shared Water Resources. *Water International, 40*(1), 21–32.

Lee, S. (2015). Benefit Sharing in the Mekong River Basin. *Water International, 40*(1), 139–52.

LMC (2016). Sanya Declaration of the First Lancang-Mekong Cooperation (LMC) Leaders' Meeting (adopted March 23, 2016).

Lowi, M. R. (1995). *Water and Power: The politics of a scarce resource in the Jordan River basin.* Cambridge: Cambridge University Press.

McCaffrey, S. (1990). Sixth Report on the Law of the Non-Navigational Uses of International Watercourses (A/CN.4/427). *Yearbook of the International Law Commission, 11*(1), 41–82.

McCaffrey, S. (2014). The Convention Enters into Force. *Environmental Policy and Law, 44*(4), 351–6.

McCaffrey, S. (2015). The 1997 UN Convention: Compatibility and Complementarity. In A. Tanzi, O. McIntyre, A. Kolliopoulos, A. Rieu-Clarke & R. Kinna (Eds.), *The UNECE Convention on the Protection and Use of Transboundary Watercourses and International Lakes: Its Contribution to International Water Cooperation* (pp. 51–9). Leiden: Brill-Nijhoff.

McCaffrey, S. (2017). The Evolution of International Water Law. In A. Rieu-Clarke, A. Allan & S. Hendry (Eds.), *Routledge Handbook of Water Law and Policy* (pp. 205–16). Abingdon: Routledge.

McCaffrey, S. (2019). *The Law of International Watercourses* (3 ed.). Oxford: Oxford University Press.

McCaffrey, S. & Sinjela, M. (1998). The 1997 United Nations Convention on International Watercourses. *The American Journal of International Law, 92*(1), 97–107.

McIntyre, O. (2007). *Environmental Protection of International Watercourses under International Law.* Abingdon/Burlington: Ashgate Publishing.

McIntyre, O. (2015a). Benefit-Sharing and Upstream/Downstream Cooperation for Ecological Protection of Transboundary Waters: Opportunities for China as an Upstream State. *Water International, 40*(1), 48–70.

McIntyre, O. (2015b). The Principle of Equitable and Reasonable Utilisation. In A. Tanzi, O. McIntyre, A. Kolliopoulos, A. Rieu-Clarke & R. Kinna (Eds.), *The UNECE Convention on the Protection and Use of Transboundary Watercourses and International Lakes: Its Contribution to International Water Cooperation* (pp. 146–59). Leiden: Brill-Nijhoff.

McIntyre, O. (2015c). The UNECE Water Convention and the Human Right to Access to Water: The Protocol on Water and Health. In A. Tanzi, O. McIntyre, A. Kolliopoulos & A. Rieu-Clarke & R. Kinna (Eds.), *The UNECE Convention on the Protection and Use of Transboundary Watercourses and International Lakes: Its Contribution to International Water Cooperation* (pp. 345–66). Leiden: Brill-Nijhoff.

McIntyre, O. (2017). Substantive Rules of International Water Law. In A. Rieu-Clarke, A. Allan & S. Hendry (Eds.), *Routledge Handbook of Water Law and Policy.* Abingdon: Routledge.

McKenzie, S. (2013). A River Runs Through It: The Future of the Columbia River Treaty, Water Rights, Development and Climate Change. *Georgia State University Law Review, 29*(4), 922–58.

Mehling, M. (2012). Enforcing Compliance in an Evolving Climate Regime. In J. Brunée, M. Doelle & L. Rajamani (Eds.), *Promoting Compliance in an Evolving Climate Regime* (pp. 194–215). Cambridge: Cambridge University Press.

MRC (1995). Agreement on the Cooperation for the Sustainable Development of the Mekong River Basin (adopted April 5, 1995).

MRC (2017). The Effects of Chinese Dams on Water Flows in the Lower Mekong Basin. *Mekong River Commission* – June 6. Retrieved from www.mrcmekong.org/news-and-events/news/the-effects-of-chinese-dams-on-water-flows-in-the-lower-mekong-basin/

MRC (2019). State of the Basin Report 2018. Retrieved from www.mrcmekong.org/assets/Publications/SOBR-v8_Final-for-web.pd

The Nation (2020). China Increases Water Release to Help Mekong Basin Countries. *The Nation Thailand* – March 20. Retrieved from www.nationthailand.com/news/30381002

Paisley, R. (2002). Adversaries into Partners: International Water Law and the Equitable Sharing of Downstream Benefits. *Melbourne Journal of International Law*, *3*, 280–300.

Paulus, A. (2011). Reciprocity Revisited. In R. G. Ulrich Fastenrath, D. E. Khan, A. Paulus, S. von Schorlemer & C.Vedder (Eds.), *From Bilateralism to Community Interest: Essays in Honour of Bruno Simma* (pp. 114–37). Oxford: Oxford University Press.

Pauwelyn, J. (2003). A Typology of Multilateral Treaty Obligations: Are WTO Obligations Bilateral or Collective in Nature?. *European Journal of International Law*, *14*(5), 907–51.

Posner, E. A. (2012). Human Rights, The Laws of War and Reciprocity. *Law and Ethics of Human Rights*, *6*(2), 147–71.

Ptak, T. & Hommel, D. (2016). The Trans-Political Nature of Southwest China's Energy Conduit, Yunnan Province. *Geopolitics*, *21*(3), 556–78.

Räsänen, T. A., Someth, P., Lauri, H., Koponen, J., Sarkkula, J. & Kummu, M. (2017). Observed River Discharge Changes due to Hydropower Operations in the Upper Mekong Basin. *Journal of Hydrology*, *545*, 28–41.

Rieu-Clarke, A. (2015). Remarks on the Drafting History of the Convention. In A. Tanzi, O. McIntyre, A. Kolliopoulos, A. Rieu-Clarke & R. Kinna (Eds.), *The UNECE Convention on the Protection and Use of Transboundary Watercourses and International Lakes: Its Contribution to International Water Cooperation* (pp. 3–14). Leiden: Brill-Nijhoff.

Rieu-Clarke, A. & Loures, F. R. (2009). Still Not in Force: Should States Support the 1997 UN Watercourses Convention?. *RECIEL*, *18*(2), 185–7.

Sadoff, C. W. & Grey, D. (2005). Cooperation on International Rivers. *Water International*, *30*(4), 420–7.

Salman, S. (2007a). The Helsinki Rules, The UN Watercourses Convention and the Berlin Rules: Perspectives on International Water Law. *Water Resources Development*, *34*(4), 625–40.

Salman, S. (2007b). The United Nations Watercourses Convention Ten Years Later: Why Has its Entry into Force Proven Difficult? *Water International*, *32*(1), 1–15.

Salman, S. (2010). Downstream Riparians can also Harm Upstream Riparians: The Concept of Foreclosure of Future Uses. *Water International*, *35*(4), 350–64.

Schmeier, S. (2013). Governing International Watercourses: River Basin Organizations and the Sustainable Government of Internationally Shared Rivers and Lakes. New York: Earthscan.

Simma, B. (1989). Bilateralism and Community Interest in the Law of State Responsibility. In Y. Dinstein & M. Tabory (Eds.), *International Law at a Time of Perplexity* (pp. 821–44). Dordrecht, The Netherlands: Martinus Nijhoff.

Simma, B. (1994). From Bilateralism to Community Interest. *Recueil des cours 250*, 221–384.

Simma, B. (2008). Reciprocity. In R. Wolfrum (Ed.), *Max Planck Encyclopedias of International Law*, Oxford: Oxford University Press.

Spijkers, O., Li, X. & Dai, L. (2016). Sustainable Development in China's International and Domestic Water Law. *Journal of Water Law, 24*(5–6), 207–19.

Su, Y. (2014). Contemporary Legal Analysis of China's Transboundary Water Regimes: International Law in Practice. *Water International, 39*(5), 705–24.

Su, Y. (2019). China's International Water Relations. In S. McCaffrey, C. Leb & R. T. Denoon (Eds.), *Research Handbook on International Water Law* (pp. 447–62). Cheltenham: Edward Elgar.

Tanzi, A. (2010). Reducing the Gap between International Water Law and Human Rights Law: The UNECE Protocol on Water and Health. *International Community Law Review, 12*, 267–85.

Tanzi, A. (2015). *The Economic Commission for Europe Water Convention and the United Nations Watercourses Convention: An Analysis of their Harmonized Contribution to International Water Law (ECE/MP.WAT/42)*, UNECE. Retrieved from www.unwater.org/app/uploads/2017/05/ece_mp.wat_42_eng_web.pdf

Tanzi, A. & Arcari, M. (2001). *The United Nations Convention on the Law of International Watercourses: A Framework for Sharing*. The Hague: Kluwer Law International.

Tanzi, A. & Kolliopoulos, A. (2015). The No-Harm Rule. In A. Tanzi, O. McIntyre, A. Kolliopoulos, A. Rieu-Clarke & R. Kinna (Eds.), *The UNECE Convention on the Protection and Use of Transboundary Watercourses and International Lakes Its Contribution to International Water Cooperation* (pp. 133–45). Leiden: Brill-Nijhoff.

Tarlock, A. D. & Wouters, P. (2007). Are Shared Benefits of International Waters an Equitable Apportionment? *Colorado Journal of International Environmental Law, 18*(3), 523–36.

Tian, F. & Liu, H. (2016). "China's Water Hegemony in Asia" or "Shared Rivers, Shared Futures": Which? *Embassy of the People's Republic of China in the Kingdom of Thailand* – June 27. Retrieved from http://th.china-embassy.org/eng/ztbd/t1384905.htm

Tiezzi, S. (2016). Facing Mekong Drought, China to Release Water from Yunnan Dam. *The Diplomat* – March 16. Retrieved from http://thediplomat.com/2016/03/facing-mekong-drought-china-to-release-water-from-yunnan-dam/

Trombitcaia, I. & Koeppel, S. (2015). From a Regional towards a Global Instrument – The 2003 Amendment to the UNECE Water Convention. In A. Tanzi, O. McIntyre, A. Kolliopoulos, A. Rieu-Clarke & R. Kinna (Eds.), *The UNECE Convention on the Protection and Use of Transboundary Watercourses and International Lakes: Its Contribution to International Water Cooperation* (pp. 15–31). Leiden: Brill-Nijhoff.

Tumen (China-DPRK-Mongolia-ROK-Russia) (1994). Memorandum of Understanding on Environmental Principles Governing the Tumen River Economic Development Area and Northeast Asia (adopted January 1, 1994).

UNCESCR (Committee on Economic, Social and Cultural Rights) (2002). *General Comment No. 15: The Right to Water*, E/c.12/2002/11 (November 29, 2002). Retrieved from https://documents-dds-ny.un.org/doc/UNDOC/GEN/G03/402/29/pdf/G0340229.pdf?OpenElement

UNECE (1999). *Protocol on Water and Health to the 1992 Convention on the Protection and Use of Transboundary Watercourses and International Lakes*, MP.WAT/2000/1 (June 17, 1999). Retrieved from https://documents-dds-ny.un.org/doc/UNDOC/GEN/G99/329/20/pdf/G9932920.pdf?OpenElement

UNECE (2013). *Guide to Implementing the Water Convention*, ECE/MP.WAT/39 (September 2013). Retrieved from www.unece.org/fileadmin/DAM/env/water/publications/WAT_Guide_to_implementing_Convention/ECE_MP.WAT_39_Guide_to_implementing_water_convention_small_size_ENG.pdf

UNGA (1970). *Progressive Development and Codification of the Rules of International Law Relating to International Watercourses*, General Assembly Resolution 2669 (XXV) (December 9, 1970). Retrieved from www.un.org/ga/search/view_doc.asp?symbol=A/Res/2669(XXV)

UNGA (1996a). *Summary Record of the 12th Meeting, 6th Committee*, A/C.6/51/SR.12 (October 7, 1996). Retrieved from https://documents-dds-ny.un.org/doc/UNDOC/GEN/N96/812/88/pdf/N9681288.pdf?OpenElement

UNGA (1996b). *Summary Record of the 15th Meeting, 6th Committee*, A/C.6/51/SR.15 (October 8, 1996). Retrieved from https://documents-dds-ny.un.org/doc/UNDOC/GEN/N96/813/24/pdf/N9681324.pdf?OpenElement

UNGA (1996c). *Summary Record of the 17th Meeting, 6th Committee*, A/C.6/51/SR.17 (October 9, 1996). Retrieved from https://documents-dds-ny.un.org/doc/UNDOC/GEN/N96/813/48/pdf/N9681348.pdf?OpenElement

UNGA (1996d). *Summary Record of the 20th Meeting, 6th Committee*, A/C.6/51/SR.20 (October 14, 1996). Retrieved from https://documents-dds-ny.un.org/doc/UNDOC/GEN/N96/814/03/pdf/N9681403.pdf?OpenElement

UNGA (1997a). *99th Plenary Meeting, United Nations General Assembly*, A/51/PV.99 (May 21, 1997). Retrieved from https://documents-dds-ny.un.org/doc/UNDOC/GEN/N97/855/72/pdf/N9785572.pdf?OpenElement

UNGA (1997b). *Summary Record of the 61st Meeting, 6th Committee*, A/C.6/51/SR.61 (April 4, 1997). Retrieved from https://documents-dds-ny.un.org/doc/UNDOC/GEN/N97/810/58/pdf/N9781058.pdf?OpenElement

UNGA (1997c). *Summary Record of the First Part of the 62nd Meeting, 6th Committee*, A/C.6/51/SR.62 (April 4, 1997). Retrieved from https://documents-dds-ny.un.org/doc/UNDOC/GEN/N97/810/69/pdf/N9781069.pdf?OpenElement

UNGA (2010). *64/292 The Human Right to Water and Sanitation*, A/RES/64/292 (August 3, 2010). Retrieved from https://documents-dds-ny.un.org/doc/UNDOC/GEN/N09/479/35/pdf/N0947935.pdf?OpenElement

UNHRC (2004). *General Comment No. 31 – The Nature of the General Legal Obligation Imposed on States Parties to the Covenant*, CCPR/C/21/Rev.1/Add.13 (May 26, 2004). Retrieved from https://documents-dds-ny.un.org/doc/UNDOC/GEN/G04/419/56/pdf/G0441956.pdf?OpenElement

UNHRC (2010). *Resolution adopted by the Human Rights Council 15/9 – Human Rights and Access to Safe Drinking Water and Sanitation*, A/HRC/RES/15/9 (October 6, 2010).

Retrieved from https://documents-dds-ny.un.org/doc/UNDOC/GEN/G10/166/33/pdf/G1016633.pdf?OpenElement

UNTC (1992). Convention on the Protection and Use of Transboundary Watercourses and International Lakes: Status. *United Nations Treaty Collection.* Retrieved from https://treaties.un.org/pages/ViewDetails.aspx?src=TREATY&mtdsg_no=XXVII-5&chapter=27&clang=_en

UNTC (1997). Convention on the Law of the Non-Navigational Uses of International Watercourses: Status. *UN Treaty Collection.* Retrieved from https://treaties.un.org/Pages/ViewDetails.aspx?src=TREATY&mtdsg_no=XXVII-12&chapter=27&clang=_en#1

VCDR (1961). Vienna Convention on Diplomatic Relations (adopted April 18, 1961; entered into force April 24, 1964).

VCLT (1969). Vienna Convention on the Law of Treaties (adopted May 23, 1969; entered into force January 27, 1980).

Vinogradov, S. & Wouters, P. (2013). *Sino-Russian Transboundary Waters: A Legal Perspective on Cooperation.* Institute for Security & Development Policy. Retrieved from http://isdp.eu/content/uploads/images/stories/isdp-main-pdf/2013-vinogradov-wouters-sino-russian-transboundary-waters-legal-perspective.pdf

Water Convention (1992). Convention on the Protection and Use of Transboundary Watercourses and International Lakes (adopted on March 17, 1992; entered into force October 6, 1996).

Watercourses Convention (1997). United Nations Convention on the Law of Non-Navigational Uses of International Watercourses (adopted on May 21, 1997; entered into force August 17, 2014).

Wouters, P. (1999). The Legal Response to International Water Conflicts: The UN Watercourses Convention and Beyond. *German Yearbook of International Law, 42,* 293–336.

Wouters, P. (2014). The Yin and Yang of International Water Law: China's Transboundary Water Practice and the Changing Contours of Sovereignty. *RECIEL, 23*(1), 67–75.

Wouters, P. & Chen, H. (2013). China's "Soft-Path" to Transboundary Water Cooperation Examined in the Light of Two UN Global Water Conventions–Exploring the "Chinese Way." *Journal of Water Law, 22*(6), 229–47.

Wouters, P. & Rieu-Clarke, A. (2001). The Role of International Water Law in Promoting Sustainable Development. *Journal of Water Law, 12*(5), 281–3.

Xie, L. & Jia, S. (2018). *China's International Transboundary Rivers: Politics, Security and Diplomacy of Shared Water Resources.* Abingdon/New York: Routledge.

Zeitoun, M. (2015). The Relevance of International Water Law to Later-Developing Upstream States. *Water International, 40*(7), 949–68.

Yihdego, Z. & Rieu-Clarke, A. (2016). An Exploration of Fairness in International Law through the Blue Nile and GERD. *Water International, 41*(4), 528–49.

Zhong, Y., Tian, F., Hu, H., Grey, D. & Gilmont, M. (2016). Rivers and Reciprocity: Perceptions and Policy on International Watercourses. *Water Policy, 18*(3), 803–25.

5 The duty to cooperate in the global water conventions

Rules of procedure, dispute settlement and self-help mechanisms

In 2016, the United Nations Security Council discussed, for the very first time, the multi-faceted relationship between water, peace and security, recognizing the connection between transboundary water cooperation and the prevention of conflict (UNSC 2016: 4). China too recognized the need for cooperation on transboundary waters, indicating that "dialogue and cooperation must be strengthened in order to appropriately address issues related to transboundary water resources," that "transboundary water resources affect the common well-being of countries on the lower and upper reaches of river basins," and that it is "committed to strengthening coordination and communication so as to promote mutually beneficial cooperation" (UNSC 2016: 16). Cooperation, "where parties agree to work together to produce new gains for each of the participants unavailable to them by unilateral action, at some cost" (Zartman & Touval 2011: 1), is the "cornerstone of modern international law" (Wouters 2013: 16) and of the utmost importance to transboundary water management. Reciprocity and expectations of reciprocal exchange, either positive or negative, is at the heart of cooperation, alongside the allocation of benefits (Zartman & Touval 2011). In the law of international watercourses, benefits are allocated and harm is mitigated via the substantive rules of equitable and reasonable use and the due diligence obligation not to cause significant harm. Chapter 4 examined the substantive rules of the law of international watercourses, providing an interpretation using the lens of reciprocity. These rules, however, are enacted through various avenues of cooperation via the procedural rules, including information sharing, prior notification and consultation which "provide the practical means for implementing the substantive rules and establish an operational framework" (Wouters 2013: 20).

This chapter aims to bridge the substantive rules with their procedural counterparts including information exchange, prior notification and consultation, via the duty to cooperate as found in the 1997 United Nations Convention on the Law of the Non-navigational Uses of International Watercourses (Watercourses Convention), 1992 United Nations Economic Commission for Europe (UNECE) Convention on the Protection and Use of Transboundary Watercourses and International Lakes (Water Convention), and China's treaty practice. In doing so, it aims to illustrate that they too follow a reciprocal structure. While only one of these procedural rules – prior notification – is considered to be a rule of customary international law, each of them is fundamental in upholding the customary rules of equitable and reasonable use and the due diligence obligation not to cause significant harm. Whereas the inclusion of the substantive rules in China's transboundary water treaty practice is uneven, they are prominent in China's practice across its transboundary waters, occasionally acting as the first incremental step towards greater cooperation and trust-building. While these procedural rules act as mechanisms of conflict prevention, where cooperation nonetheless fails, reciprocity can still prevail through a variety of dispute settlement mechanisms, albeit only where there is a foundation of mutual consent. There is growing practice in this regard internationally, but limited practice between China and its neighbours.

In instances where dispute settlement is not available or may be ineffective, how might states act to enforce these norms and bring states back into compliance? Within international law states may, within limits, turn to additional legal mechanisms such as retorsion, non-performance, suspension and countermeasures within which "reciprocity has been crystallized" (ICJ 2011: 59). State responsibility and self-help measures have been utilized in other areas of international law; however, the use of such mechanisms in relation to transboundary waters has been incredibly limited and very little research has been conducted on the subject (for example, McIntyre 2019). Thus, the chapter will explore the limited use of such mechanisms in the law of international watercourses, and potential explanations for this. In terms of the reciprocal structure of international law, the possibility that the duty to cooperate is an emerging obligation *erga omnes* coupled with the well-established rules of customary and treaty law and practice in this field is particularly helpful in determining the contours of the use of self-help measures in transboundary waters, and will be the primary focus.

The legal notion of reciprocity and the duty to cooperate

Given that reciprocity establishes a balance of rights and duties, it can act as a catalyst for cooperation. The duty to cooperate is the very foundation of international law, firmly reflected in the United Nations (UN) Charter most prominently in Article 1, which sets out the purpose of the UN. This includes the maintenance of international peace and security, the development of friendly relations, the achievement of international cooperation in solving international problems, and the harmonization of state actions to achieve these goals (UN Charter 1945: art. 1). The duty to cooperate has since appeared in a series of prominent UN documents, most notably the 1970 Declaration on Principles of International Law Concerning Friendly Relations and Cooperation among States which reaffirms the Charter. It is also found in a series of treaties, particularly multilateral environmental agreements, including the 1992

Convention on Biological Diversity, found throughout the 1992 UN Framework Convention on Climate Change, and UN Convention on the Law of the Sea, among others (Leb 2013). It can also be considered a rule of customary international law, as it is "not only necessary, but is probably now required by general international law" (McCaffrey 2019: 532). This is an abstract obligation, but it finds meaning in other principles such as sovereign equality, good faith and reciprocity. Similar to the Five Principles of Peaceful Coexistence discussed in Chapter 2, the duty to cooperate occurs between equals based upon "mutual respect for one another's territorial integrity" (Leb 2013: 82) as they aim to achieve mutual benefit. Applying to all states equally, it acts as a bridge between the substantive and procedural, providing the "fulcrum for balancing the broad spectrum of potential oppositional forces" (Wouters 2014: 68).

This customary duty is absolutely necessary for the implementation of the fundamental pillars of the law of international watercourses, particularly the customary rules of equitable and reasonable use and the due diligence obligation not to cause significant harm. Articulated in Article 8 of the Watercourses Convention, the general duty to cooperate stipulates that "watercourse states shall cooperate on the basis of sovereign equality, territorial integrity, mutual benefit and good faith in order to attain optimal utilization and adequate protection of the international watercourse" (1997: art. 8). Unlike the duty to cooperate in the Watercourses Convention, the Water Convention explicitly includes reciprocity as a fundamental principle while providing "clearer guidance on how the duty to cooperate operates to protect the environment within the watercourses context" (Wouters & Leb 2015: 291). Articulated in multiple provisions, primarily in Article 9(1) but also the Preamble and Article 2(6), it indicates that states:

> shall on the basis of equality and reciprocity enter into bilateral or multilateral or other arrangements, where these do not yet exist, or adapt existing ones, where necessary to eliminate the contradictions with the basic principles of this Convention, in order to define their mutual relations and conduct regarding the prevention, control and reduction of transboundary impact.
>
> (Water Convention 1992: art. 9(1))

It goes on in Article 9(2–5) to state that such cooperative arrangements must take into consideration all aspects of the implementation of the Convention, ranging from the establishment of joint bodies, information sharing, warning procedures, joint monitoring and even the protection of the marine environment.

Beyond the preamble, as discussed in Chapter 2, China's treaties often include provisions concerning the duty to cooperate as a primary guiding principle. For example, Article 2 of the 2001 China–Kazakhstan Agreement states that "in the use of transboundary rivers" states shall "closely cooperate in a sincere, neighborly and friendly manner." The "bridging" aspect of the duty to cooperate is clearly illustrated in the 1994 China–Mongolia Agreement, which links cooperation to equitable and reasonable utilization in Article 2, going on to state that "for the implementation of the cooperation provided for in Article 2" the parties will conduct cooperation in a series of areas which represent procedural rules (1994: art. 2). Although there are no agreements or related documents between China and its southwestern neighbours that explicitly provide for the duty to cooperate, they do recognize this cooperation as evidenced through the presence of various procedural rules, as discussed next.

Understanding the procedural and dispute settlement rules through the lens of reciprocity

The duty to cooperate is operationalized through a series of procedural rules, including information exchange, prior notification and consultation in which reciprocity plays a pivotal role. Of these rules, only prior notification is considered customary international law, as elaborated on in the *Pulp Mills Case* (ICJ 2010; McCaffrey 2019; McIntyre 2011). These procedural rules guide a process of cooperation based upon reciprocal rights and duties of the parties aimed towards finding, reaching and maintaining an equitable and reasonable allocation of beneficial uses, as well as preventing the occurrence of significant harm. These rules work to avoid conflict; if conflict does occur, however, states have a series of mechanisms at their disposal to settle their disputes peacefully. Thus, this section will analyse these procedural and dispute settlement mechanisms found within both global water conventions, the Watercourses Convention and the Water Convention, through the lens of reciprocity, seeking to illuminate how they work in practice.

The procedural rules of the Watercourses Convention

Article 9 of the Watercourses Convention provides that "States shall on a regular basis exchange readily available data and information on the condition of the watercourse." Such an obligation implies an "ongoing and systematic process" (ILC 1994) of reciprocation in the sense that each party has the duty to provide as well as the corresponding right to receive information. When projects are planned states are required to inform their riparian neighbours of both its positive and negative effects (1997: art. 11). If, however, the project is likely to have "a significant adverse effect upon other watercourse States" (1997: art. 12), then parties must follow a series of procedures designed to avoid a dispute, as set out in Articles 12 through 18. The standard of a "significant adverse effect" is lower than that of "significant harm" found in Article 7, assuring that states do not face a situation where they must admit that such planned measures will cause significant harm to the other states (ILC 1994). This lower standard also ensures that the duty applies to all equally, as "adverse impacts" could take on various forms which impact both upstream and downstream states. This prior notification triggers a back and forth exchange between riparians, with states obligated to reply to said notification within a six-month period (1997: art. 12, 13 & 15). All the while, the notifying state must not proceed with its planned measures, and ought to provide additional information requested by the notified state (1997: art. 14). If the notified state does not participate in the exchange and does not reply, then the notifying state may proceed with its planned measures according to the previously provided notification (1997: art. 16). If the planned measures under discussion are found to violate the substantive rules of equitable and reasonable use and the due diligence obligation not to cause significant harm (1997: art. 5–7), then Article 17 obligates the notifying and notified state to "enter into consultations and, if necessary, negotiations with a view to arriving at an equitable resolution of the situation." These consultations, based upon mutual consideration of the rights and interests of the other in good faith, represent a reciprocal process in which states make claims and then reciprocate until a compromise is reached. If a state believes that their riparian neighbour is planning measures that may have a significant adverse effect upon them, then they may initiate this reciprocal process by submitting a request that the state applies Article 12, along with the rationale for such a request (1997: art. 18).

The procedural rules of the Water Convention

So as to "ensure effective protection of transboundary waters, management of water quality and quantity as well as the prevention, control and reduction of transboundary impacts" (UNECE 2013), Article 13 of the Water Convention states that riparian parties "shall, within the framework of relevant agreements or other arrangements according to Article 9 of this Convention, exchange reasonable available data" (1992: art. 13). Thus, all parties have the right to receive such information as is reasonably available, and the corresponding duty to provide said information. Such information, at a minimum, is to concern environmental conditions, experience in the use and application of the "best available technology," emissions and monitoring information, planned measures to "prevent, control and reduce transboundary impact," as well as permits and regulations concerning waste-water emissions (1992: art. 13(1a-e)). Given that parties to the Convention are under a general duty to share information under Article 6, however, this list is non-exhaustive and parties are encouraged to expand upon these areas of information sharing (UNECE 2013). Such reciprocal information sharing, however, only refers to information that is reasonably available, and in the case of requests for information that is not reasonably available the state "shall endeavour to comply with the request" but may request compensation (1992: art. 13(3)). Much of this information collection and sharing occurs within the joint bodies established under Article 9(2), who act to "collect, compile and evaluate data" as well as to inventory and exchange information regarding sources of pollution (1992: art. 9 (2a & c)).

Article 14 requires states to notify riparian parties of any "critical situation" that has transboundary impact (1992: art. 14), however, unlike the Watercourses Convention, the Water Convention does not contain a provision which expressly provides the duty to notify of planned measures. States would, however, still be governed by the rule as it is customary law (ICJ 2010; McCaffrey 2019; McIntyre 2011). Although there is no explicit duty within the Water Convention, it has been incorporated within other articles. For example, as part of the list of information to be exchanged between riparian parties, states also ought to share information regarding "measures taken and planned to be taken to prevent, control and reduce transboundary impact" (1992: art. 13(d)). Consultation, however, is not specifically tied to such notification or necessarily to any occurrence of transboundary impact (UNECE 2013), as Article 10 requires that consultations are to "be held between the Riparian Parties on the basis of reciprocity, good faith and good-neighbourliness, at the request of any such parties" and will occur within the framework of the joint bodies established between the riparian parties, if they exist. Thus, states can at any time request consultations, and the other state "cannot in principle ignore it" (UNECE 2013). In terms of their reciprocal obligation, states have the right to request and the duty to reply, making consultations a reciprocal process. Given that they are based on the principle of reciprocity as well as good faith and good-neighbourliness, such consultations are not simply a "formalistic exchange of views, but a substantive process" (UNECE 2013: 78) where states take the interests of the other into account. All of these procedural rules are enhanced by the Meeting of the Parties, established under Article 17. These meetings, held every three years with the first held in 1997, seek to "review the implementation" through the review of policies, exchange of information regarding best practices, seek the assistance of other UNECE bodies, propose and adopt amendments, and "undertake any additional action that may be required for the achievement of the purposes of this Convention" (1992: art. 17).

Dispute settlement mechanisms of the of the global water conventions

As set out in the UN Charter, Article 2(3), provides that states must settle their disputes peacefully. In order to do so, there are a variety of mechanisms available for them, including diplomatic methods such as negotiation, good offices and mediation, fact-finding, and conciliation, each of which represent a reciprocal exchange of claims leading to compromise. Beyond these diplomatic measures, states can also resort to centralized methods of dispute resolution such as the ICJ or arbitration. Resort to such measures, however, requires the consent of the parties to the dispute, often based on a reciprocity clause found in a treaty. For example, consent to the jurisdiction of the ICJ is based upon a reciprocal jurisdiction clause found in Article 36(2) of the Statute of the ICJ. It states that parties may "declare that they recognize as compulsory *ipso facto* and without special agreement, *in relation to any other state accepting the same obligation*, the jurisdiction of the Court [...]" (ICJ 1945: art 36(2)). Thus, states can consent to the jurisdiction of the court unconditionally based upon reciprocity (ICJ 1945: art. 36(3)), such that a state will consent to its jurisdiction so long as the other party of the dispute has also consented. Furthermore, the source of this consent might be contained in bilateral or multilateral treaties.

When disputes arise, both the Watercourses Convention and Water Convention provide a process that state parties can pursue to peacefully settle their disputes. If the dispute cannot be settled via negotiation, then the Watercourses Convention makes available a series of other mechanisms including good offices, mediation, conciliation, or the settlement of disputes through a joint watercourse body (1997: art. 33(1 & 2)). If such mechanisms are unsuccessful, then after six months the case "shall be submitted, at the request of any of the parties to the dispute, to impartial fact finding," involving a third party (1997: art. 33(3)). Although the Water Convention does not explicitly mention these diplomatic methods of dispute settlement, they are available as Article 22(1) states that if a dispute arises the parties to the dispute "shall seek a solution by *negotiation or by any other means of dispute settlement* acceptable to the parties to the dispute" (Water Convention 1992). This also refers to dispute settlement through the joint bodies that parties to the Convention "shall provide for the establishment of," as found in Article 9(2).

Despite the fact that the Water Convention does not require mandatory impartial fact-finding like the Watercourses Convention, both permit parties to refer their dispute to the ICJ or to arbitration based upon a reciprocal jurisdiction clause similar to that found in the Statute of the ICJ (Water Convention 1992: art. 22; Watercourses Convention 1997: art. 33(10)). Many states, including China, take issue with mandatory fact-finding and have not consented to the jurisdiction of the ICJ, and it is clear that the inclusion of these mechanisms may act as a "deterrent in the way to ratification of that Convention for States that are prepared to accept third-party dispute settlement procedures only on an optional basis" (Tanzi & Contartese 2015: 325). These third-party mechanisms, however, often aim to support negotiations by collecting new information, or by placing pressure on the parties to reach a solution (Tanzi & Milano 2013). This was the case in the *Gabčíkovo-Nagymaros Case* which referred the states to further negotiations in order to find an agreeable solution (ICJ 1997a), and *Pulp Mills Case* which reminded the parties of their cooperation via the joint mechanism Comisión Administradora del Río Uruguay (CARU) such that they have been able to find "appropriate solutions to their differences within its framework without feeling the need to resort to the judicial settlement of disputes" through the ICJ in the past (ICJ 2010: 176). As such, the Watercourses Convention and arguably the Water Convention provide an open-ended framework that caters to states who consent, based on reciprocity, to mechanisms of third-party dispute settlement. Those who do not consent, however, can continue to find a solution through consultation and negotiation or through a specific agreement for dispute settlement (Tanzi & Contartese 2015: 176).

Although the process of dispute settlement is similar in both Conventions, the Water Convention provides an alternative method of dispute avoidance, via the innovative Implementation Committee. Established in 2012 at the Meeting of the Parties in Rome (UNECE 2012a), the Committee consists of nine members who possess legal and/or scientific expertise (UNECE 2012b: sect. 2(3–4)). With the aim to "facilitate, promote and safeguard the implementation and application" of the Water Convention (UNECE 2012b: sect. 1(1)), the mechanisms provide an "alternative to adjudication which may combine the features of mediation [and] conciliation," providing advice on any difficulties parties may have with implementation or compliance with the Convention (Tanzi & Contartese 2015: 326). As a mechanism that is intended to be "simple, non-confrontational, non-adversarial, transparent, supportive and cooperative in nature" (UNECE 2012b: sect. 1(2)), issues may be brought to the Committee by parties, either individually or jointly, at the request of the Meeting of the Parties, and by the Committee itself (Lammers 2014). Upon hearing a request, the Committee can provide advice, suggestions, assistance and help by facilitating financial or technical assistance (UNECE 2012b). Through such a mechanism, state parties have an alternative body in which, like the aforementioned dispute settlement methods, they can follow a reciprocal path to compromise, and given that such a process "shall not be regarded as alleging non-compliance" (UNECE 2012b: sect. 5(18)) states may be more inclined to do so.

China's transboundary water treaty practice: reciprocity in the procedural rules

In order to implement the guiding principle of cooperation, China's transboundary treaties contain a series of procedural rules concerning information sharing, prior notification and dispute settlement.

Information sharing

Information sharing provisions are quite common in China's transboundary treaties, often requiring a reciprocal exchange of information between China and its riparian neighbours. The 2001 China–Kazakhstan Agreement, Article 6 provides for information sharing between the parties, indicating that "the parties shall agree and determine the content of, quantity of, and times for exchange of data information" (2001: art. 6). The 1994 China–Mongolia Agreement, Article 3 indicates that the parties may conduct "technological exchanges," which include "exchanges of technical materials, information and maps within the framework of cooperation" (1994: art. 3). This exchange is conducted in support of Article 2, which lists activities for the realization of "protection and equitable and rational use of transboundary waters" (China–Mongolia 1994: art. 2 & 3). China shares information with India regarding the Langqen Zanbgo-Sutlej River according to a 2005 MoU which has been renewed and is still in effect (MWR 2014). These states also share information concerning the Yaluzangbu-Brahmaputra River during the flood season as of 2002 after signing an MoU that has been renewed multiple times (MWR 2014). According to the 2013 Implementation Plan, this requires a reciprocal exchange of information where China provides hydrological information during the flood season and India provides information on "data utilization in flood forecasting and mitigation" as well as a payment of US$850,000 each April (China–India 2014: art. 11). In spite of ongoing border issues between China and India as earlier discussed in Chapter 2, they have renewed these information-sharing agreements multiple times. After the withdrawal of forces from Doklam, the two parties went on to renew this information-sharing agreement in 2018, even expanding the scope of information sharing ever so slightly to include the sharing of information during the flood season and also when the water levels rise above a "mutually agreed level during the non-flood season" (China–India 2018). The global water conventions offer a reciprocal information-sharing obligation; however, unilateral information sharing is common in transboundary water agreements across the world, indicating that states may be more interested in sharing information to prevent harm (Leb 2019). Even though much of the cooperation on China's transboundary waters takes place in a reciprocal manner, China also unilaterally shares information with Bangladesh as well as the Lancang-Mekong countries through the MRC. Such unilateral information sharing could be viewed as a gesture of goodwill, the first concession in a longer process of cooperation and trust-building conducted in the hopes that the other riparians will also make concessions, perhaps resulting in a formalized agreement. Whereas China shares information with India reciprocally for information or payment, China unilaterally shares hydrological information with Bangladesh, as the 2010 Bangladesh–China Joint Statement calls for the two countries to cooperate on hydrological data sharing "in view of its necessity to the disaster reduction in Bangladesh". Although China only has observer status at the MRC and is not a party to the treaty, it signed an agreement in 2002, renewed in 2008, 2013 and 2019 (MRC 2019b), to provide hydrological information during the flood season (MRC 2008) without payment or the explicit obligation to exchange similar information. In 2020, China committed itself to providing hydrological information year round (LMC 2020).

Prior notification

China's treaties make no mention of or provide very limited obligations to prior notification (Su 2014), in line with China's stance on state sovereignty (Wouters & Chen 2013). Some treaties do, however, identify specific areas and activities that require mutual agreement. For example, Article 17 of the

China–North Korea Protocol on Borderline (1964) states that engineering works which would alter the navigation channel, flow or riverbanks of the other party require notification. Furthermore, the 2009 China–Vietnam Provisional Agreement on Border Affairs has a similar provision, requiring prior agreement for activities likely to cause a negative impact on the other riparians (Wouters & Chen 2013: 237). While not within the framework of a legal regime and not in regards to planned measures, there is some practice concerning prior notification in regards to China's upstream hydropower dams on the Lancang-Mekong. In recent years, China has consistently notified downstream states through the MRC regarding the significant increase or decrease in flows from its hydropower dams that may negatively impact its downstream neighbours (For example, MRC 2018a, 2018b, 2019a, 2019c). Unlike prior notification in the global water conventions, these notifications have not yet triggered consultations regarding hydropower operations; however, they may still act to support the substantive rules, particularly the due diligence obligation not to cause significant harm.

Dispute settlement

It is well known that China does not consent to mandatory dispute settlement mechanisms or the compulsory jurisdiction of the ICJ, preferring to choose its own method of dispute settlement, most often consultation and negotiation. It even listed mandatory dispute settlement mechanisms, specifically mandatory fact-finding (Watercourses Convention 1997: art. 33(3–9)), as one of the reasons why it voted against the Watercourses Convention. In explanation, it stated that such a provision "goes against the Charter," and that the "Chinese Government favours the settlement of all disputes by peaceful means, through consultations" (UNGA 1997). This approach is exemplified in China's transboundary water treaties with Kazakhstan, Mongolia and Russia, which explicitly mention either "consultation" or "negotiation" (Su 2014: 713). With reciprocity in mind, however, it may be difficult for these states to be on equal footing during consultations given China's more powerful position, both economically and hydrologically. A strategy of issue-linkage, one in which states link their cooperation to issues beyond water resources so as to establish an exchange (Axelrod & Keohane 1985; Daoudy 2009; Ho 2017), may provide needed balance between these parties, and given the often wide scope of China's transboundary water agreements is likely to be permitted. China–Kazakhstan cooperation, for example, not only focusses on water resources, but also on energy, and anti-terrorist measures, among others (Ho 2017). Such issue-linkage potentially permits Kazakhstan to have the upper hand in some areas of cooperation but not in others, potentially balancing China's more powerful position. Issue-linkage, like reciprocity, however, can be a "double-edged sword" as upstream, more powerful states may also utilize this strategy to extract concessions from downstream states (Ho 2017: 159).

Procedural rules and the Lancang-Mekong Cooperation Mechanism

As earlier mentioned, there are signs that cooperation on China's south-western basins is improving with the launch of the Lancang-Mekong Cooperation (LMC) Mechanism. In relation to water resources, states pledge to enhance cooperation concerning the "sustainable management and utilization of water resources," as one of the multiple issue areas, including connectivity, production capacity, cross-border economic cooperation, as well as agriculture and poverty reduction (LMC 2016). In order to further cooperation in this area, the LMC includes various mechanisms which resemble procedural rules. These include policy dialogue, information sharing, technical exchange, joint research, capacity building, and emergency management (LMC 2018b: sect. 2, para. 2(5)). Information exchange is mentioned multiple times, but it is unclear how it will take place and what information will be shared among riparians. At the second LMC Leaders Meeting the tasks of this mechanism were more clearly defined and include "sharing of data and information, technical cooperation and exchanges, carrying out joint research and analysis" among others (LMC 2018b: sect. II, para. 2(5)). However, it is likely that such information exchange will include both quantity and quality, as the Five-Year Plan adopted by the LMC in 2018 indicates the necessity to improve monitoring in relation to water quality, and quantity in relation to flood and drought management (LMC 2018a). "Consultations" regarding joint mechanisms are not mentioned, but the term "policy dialogue" could represent a similar reciprocal process (LMC 2018b: sect. II, para. 2.5). Such an exchange of information and policy dialogue are likely to take place within the many fora and institutions established by the Mechanism. In terms of dialogue, the LMC involves regular meetings at various levels, including biannual leader's meetings, annual foreign minister's meetings, as well as senior officials and working group meetings as needed, of which one is dedicated to water resources (LMC 2016). Furthermore, a series of institutions have been or will be established to support this cooperation, including a Secretariat for each riparian country, and most importantly the Lancang-Mekong Water Resources Cooperation Centre, which serves "as a platform for LMC countries to strengthen comprehensive cooperation' in many areas, including 'data and information sharing'" (LMC 2016: para. 10). There are, however, concerns regarding the future relationship of the LMC and MRC, with some questioning whether it would disrupt or bridge regional institutions (Williams 2020). This is of particular concern regarding the procedural rules, an area of potential overlap. The two institutions, however, appear to be moving closer together. Although it clearly states that it does not "create any rights or legally binding obligations," nor does it "constitute a treaty under international law," the LMC and MRC signed an MoU in 2019 indicating that they would further cooperate in areas, including information exchange and monitoring (MRC–LMC 2019).

Self-help measures in international law and their application in the law of international watercourses

Given that there is no overarching body that can enforce international law, a series of non-centralized mechanisms are "available to states to deter and punish wrongdoing and to reward and encourage compliance [...]" (Fard 2016: 79). These mechanisms, found within the Vienna Convention on the Law of Treaties (VCLT) as well as the Draft Articles on Responsibility of States for Internationally Wrongful Acts (ARSIWA), include: 1) retorsion, 2) non-performance, 3) suspension and 4) countermeasures. In the words of Bruno Simma, these measures represent how "'raw' reciprocity has been channeled and civilized by subjecting it to legal limits" and "serves as an important deterrent and is chiefly responsible for the observance by States of international law" (ICJ 2011: 699). First, states are able to resort to retorsion, a form of retaliation which does not violate the legal rights of the other state. Such measures are largely unregulated by international law, so long as they do not result in a breach (Crawford 2013). For example, in response to generally unfriendly behaviour a state could limit diplomatic relations so long as it does not violate its responsibilities under international law. Second, when a state violates an obligation the other state can resort to non-performance, also referred to as the *exceptio inadimpleti contractus*. Such non-performance, however, is limited to the corresponding right or duty which the state has violated. Third, as permitted in VCLT, Article 60 upon a material breach states can terminate or suspend a treaty in whole or in part. That is, the injured party can temporarily suspend certain treaty obligations until the violating state complies with those obligations, or terminate the treaty in its entirety (Villiger 2009). Finally, as set out in ARSIWA, Article 22 states can take peaceful countermeasures that are unlawful which are adopted towards the non-complying state in order to induce its compliance. Such measures, previously called reprisals, are not tit-for-tat, but are peaceful "top-down" and "coercive" enforcement mechanisms which are fundamentally reciprocal in nature (Fard 2016: 87). Unlike non-performance, which permits states to violate the corresponding right or duty, countermeasures permit the state to choose which obligation they violate (Crawford 2013). These measures, however, are not without restriction and must be conducted within limits, such that: 1) they cannot involve the use of force, 2) they must be directed at the violating state, 3) they must be temporary and reversible, 4) they must be proportionate to the violation in question, and 5) the countermeasures themselves cannot violate or depart from any peremptory norms (ARSIWA 2001b: art. 49(1–3), 50, 50(1), 51 & 53). These mechanisms are utilized in other areas of international law, but they are not mentioned in either the global water conventions, nor are they mentioned in any of China's transboundary water treaties. This is not surprising, however, given China's adherence to a strong notion of sovereignty and mutual non-interference. Given the relatively few parties to both conventions, limited legal frameworks across many basins and the customary nature of various aspects of the VCLT and ARSIWA, such measures may be applicable to transboundary waters. Nevertheless, as illustrated in the *Gabčíkovo-Nagymaros Case* and *San Juan Case*, discussed below, there appears to be apprehension towards their application in regards to transboundary waters.

In 1977, Hungary and Czechoslovakia signed a treaty agreeing to establish a joint development programme and construct a series of dams on the Danube River, one in upstream Gabčíkovo, Czechoslovakia and another in downstream Nagymaros, Hungary. After a series of delays and political changes in these then communist states, Hungary suspended its part of the agreement, halting construction. Czechoslovakia then altered its plans beginning work on the so-called Variant C, so that the Gabčíkovo section of the dam could operate independently. After the separation of Czechoslovakia into two states, the dam fell under the control of Slovakia. Given heightened tensions the dispute was eventually submitted to the ICJ. In its decision, it determined that Hungary was not entitled to suspend the 1977 treaty. Nor was it entitled to suspend the 1989 works since, at the time when Hungary notified Czechoslovakia of its intent to terminate the treaty, there had not been a material breach as Variant C was only under construction and had not yet been put it into operation (ICJ 1997a). Furthermore, the Court determined that Czechoslovakia was entitled to proceed with Variant C, but was not entitled to put it into operation as this would result in diverting a large portion of the Danube waters. Although Slovakia argued its implementation of Variant C was a countermeasure against the breach by Hungary, the ICJ determined it did not meet the test of proportionality required for countermeasures since putting Variant C into operation would unilaterally control the flow of water and thus deprive Hungary of its equitable and reasonable portion of the shared waters. Ultimately, both states were ordered to return to negotiations in good faith, and to pay the other state compensation for the wrongs done. It was noted, however, that their competing claims for compensation could nullify the other, if they so agreed (ICJ 1997a).

According to the 1858 Treaty, the border between Costa Rica and Nicaragua ran along the Costa Rican side of the San Juan River, while providing Costa Rica with rights of navigation for commerce. The validation of the treaty by USA President Grover Cleveland in 1888 confirmed that the boundary line began at the mouth of the San Juan River, and laid the foundation for notification of certain works between the two countries. In 2010, Nicaragua began dredging the San Juan to improve navigability while also sending some military personnel to the area. Subsequently, that same year Costa Rica submitted a dispute to the ICJ claiming that Nicaragua had invaded its territory and illegally constructed a channel; however, Nicaragua claimed that it was clearing an existing channel. In December 2010, Costa Rica began construction of a road in the border region of its own territory, but did not notify Nicaragua of such activities. Subsequently, in 2011 Nicaragua submitted a dispute against Costa Rica claiming that construction of the road had resulted in transboundary harm. In its decision, the Court determined that Nicaragua's dredging would not risk significant transboundary harm and so did not require an environmental impact assessment (EIA), and that there was no binding obligation between the parties to notify. Nicaragua, however, was ordered to pay compensation to Costa Rica for any material damage due to its breach of Costa Rica's territorial sovereignty (ICJ 2015). No harm had occurred, but it was found that Costa Rica was obligated to determine if there was a risk of transboundary harm by conducting an EIA, and if the road construction risked significantly harming Nicaragua that it would then have to notify and consult with them. Although Nicaragua requested compensation, the Court decided that its "declaration that Costa Rica violated its obligation to conduct an environmental impact assessment is the appropriate measure of satisfaction for Nicaragua" (ICJ 2015: para. 225).

While the ICJ determined that there was a breach of the law in both cases, there is a limited application, as in the *Gabčíkovo-Nagymaros Case*, or no application, for example in the *San Juan Case*, of available self-help measures. In the *Gabčíkovo-Nagymaros Case* the parties resorted to measures of non-performance, suspension and even countermeasures, however, they were concluded to be unlawful, and it was determined that the implementation of Variant C did not meet the criteria of proportionality so as to be considered a lawful countermeasure (ICJ 1997a). It is unclear, however, how this was determined, and, given the lack of information within the judgement and Judge Vereshchetin's dissenting opinion in which he stated that he "firmly believe[s] that Czechoslovakia was fully entitled in international law to put into operation Variant C as a countermeasure so far as its partner in the Treaty persisted in violating its obligations" (ICJ 1997b: 219), it appears that there was no in-depth analysis of the proportionality of such a measure (Lefeber 1998). It could, however, be interpreted to imply that a violation of Hungary's right to an equitable and reasonable share "almost necessarily involved a disproportionate breach" when compared to Hungary's violation of the 1977 Treaty (Lammers 1998: 307). In both cases, parties were ordered to compensate the other, but ultimately were encouraged to forego their claim to compensation and continue with further negotiations. In the *San Juan Case*, it was found that Costa Rica violated its obligation to conduct an EIA, but the Court's declaration that it had breached international law was deemed enough.

Exploring the limited use of self-help measures in the context of reciprocity and the law of international watercourses

From the *Gabčíkovo-Nagymaros Case* and *San Juan Case* we can see that, even though riparian states have attempted to implement self-help measures in response to a breach, their legal application in the law of international watercourses has faced serious limitations. Furthermore, in instances where their application may be relevant, we see great apprehension in doing so. In order to explain the difficulty in implementing self-help measures in transboundary waters, scholars have pointed to the indeterminacy of the primary rules of the law of international watercourses such that determining their breach and attributing state responsibility will be incredibly difficult. Furthermore, while the procedural rules are binding, as illustrated in the above cases, their violation is not serious, often requiring compensation only (McIntyre 2019).[1] Through the lens of reciprocity, however, this trend could be interpreted as the establishment of an area of "anti-reciprocity," an area of law that is not solely governed by reciprocal concerns (Osiel 2009: 62). This notion, found in humanitarian law, is in line with recent developments in the law of international watercourses, including the possible emergence of the duty to cooperate as an obligation *erga omnes* (Wouters & Tarlock 2013). Although its status as such is highly contested, it can prove helpful in explaining the limitations surrounding self-help measures in the law of international watercourses. As such, this section will first elaborate upon the notion of reciprocity and its connection to higher-level legal norms, such as obligations *erga omnes*. It will then discuss how the duty to cooperate is a potential emerging *erga omnes* obligation, and how this might assist in determining the limitations of self-help measures in disputes concerning transboundary waters.

Reciprocity and higher-level legal norms

Whereas reciprocity aims to introduce fairness, its application is limited in some areas of law for the greater moral good, as is the case in humanitarian law. For example, after hostilities a state must release prisoners of war (POW), even if the enemy state has failed to do so. Furthermore, a state cannot target an enemy state's cultural heritage, even if the enemy state has targeted its own (Osiel 2009: 62). Reflecting the "humanisation" of humanitarian law, such a shift came about as the focus of the legal regime has shifted towards the protection of individuals, not only the interests of states (ICTY 2000: para. 518). Of course, it would be "fair" not to release POWs after hostilities have ceased if the opposing side has also not done so, but from a moral perspective this immediately appears to be wrong. This trend "marks the translation into legal norms of the 'categorical imperative'" type, where an agent ought to fulfil their obligations whether or not others do so (ICTY 2000: para. 518). In this way, such norms, referred to as obligations *erga omnes*, no longer follow a reciprocal structure of corresponding rights and duties. Obligations *erga omnes* were first clearly identified in the *Barcelona Traction Case*, where it states that

> an essential distinction should be drawn between the obligations of a State towards the international community as a whole, and those arising

> vis-à-vis another State in the field of diplomatic protection. By their very nature the former are the concern of all States. In view of the importance of the rights involved, all States can be held to have a legal interest in their protection; they are obligations *erga omnes*.
>
> (ICJ 1970: para. 33)

As such, obligations *erga omnes* are those that establish "rules which, if violated, give rise to a general right of standing – amongst all States subject to those rules – to make claims" (Byers 1997: 211). Given that international law can be conceptualized as a collection of bilateral rights and duties (Pauwelyn 2003), the establishment of an obligation *erga omnes* involves a two-step process including the establishment of a rule, and the "creation of additional bilateralizable rights and obligations" (Byers 1997: 233). This network of rights and obligations confers standing, such that "all States can be held to have a legal interest in their protection" (ICJ 1970: para. 33). As such, an obligation *erga omnes* would permit states with standing to invoke the responsibility of the violating state even if they are a non-injured state. We can understand obligations *erga omnes* to be a vast series of reciprocal rights and duties; however, their enforcement is not operationalized through reciprocity. Instead, such obligations have been altered from one which works on a bilateral, *quid pro quo* basis between states, to one which is non-bilateralizable (Fard 2016), placing limitations on the application of self-help measures. While retorsion would not be limited since such acts are lawful, this would place certain limitations on non-performance, suspension/termination as well as countermeasures. In terms of non-performance and suspension/termination of a provision or treaty, VCLT Article 60(3) permits states to suspend or terminate a treaty upon a material breach. Article 60(5), however, precludes such suspension regarding provisions that relate to the protection of the "human person in treaties of a humanitarian character" (VCLT 1969: art 60(5)). Countermeasures also face limitations when related to obligations *erga omnes*, as ARSIWA, Article 50(1) prohibits the use of countermeasures that effect human rights or humanitarian obligations.

The duty to cooperate as an emerging obligation erga omnes and its effects on the use of self-help measures

From his analysis, Ragazzi identified five common characteristics, which, although they do not necessarily entail an obligation *erga omnes*, act as a framework to assist in identifying potential *erga omnes* obligations. Accordingly, he found that obligations *erga omnes* are: 1) narrowly defined and 2) often negative obligations, which 3) include obligations or duties that are 4) derived from general rules which are *jus cogens* norms that are widely endorsed in treaty practice, and 5) which are in line with political objectives that reflect moral values (Ragazzi 2002). Given "the global nature of water resources and its unique and essential importance to life on earth" (Wouters & Tarlock 2013: 58), Wouters and Tarlock argue that the duty to cooperate in transboundary waters passes these tests and is arguably an emerging obligation *erga omnes*. In terms of transboundary waters, this would imply that even though cooperation can be operationalized through and can take on a reciprocal structure such as the various procedural rules set out in the Watercourses Convention and Water Convention, cooperation itself is no longer reciprocal. Thus, even if your neighbour chooses not to fulfil their obligations under the duty to cooperate by not acting towards the collective mutual benefit, you cannot reciprocate and ultimately aim to make them worse off. As an obligation *erga omnes* the duty goes beyond state-to-state relations and is owed to the international community as a whole, "preclud[ing] states from using their water resources in ways that are not in the interests of the global community and the world ecosystems" (Wouters & Tarlock 2013: 64). To this, Wouters and Tarlock add three corollary duties associated with this emerging obligation, including:

> 1) No state has a right to develop its waters without taking into account the interests of other watercourse states.
> 2) The duty to cooperate in the peaceful management of the world's water resources shall not be compromised by any state.
> 3) The human right to water and sanitation shall not be compromised by any state.
>
> (Wouters & Tarlock 2013: 64)

From these duties Wouters and Tarlock provide two examples of how this may function. First, unilateral development in violation of the *erga omnes* obligation would violate the principle of equitable and reasonable use. Second, the appropriate remedy for an injured state by such unilateral development may entail the "removal or significant modification of the project" (Wouters & Tarlock 2013: 64–5).

The duty to cooperate may provide the impetus for the use of various self-help measures as to ensure such cooperation, and, as earlier mentioned, its potential ascendance as an obligation *erga omnes* provides various limitations to such practices. Grounded in the human right to water, which aims to provide a baseline of protection for individuals, it is apparent that the duty to cooperate refocuses the law of international watercourses towards the human individual. This humanization is part of a growing consensus surrounding the connections between the law of international watercourses and the human right to water (Canelas de Castro 2015; Leb 2012; McIntyre 2017). While it is often discussed from a state-to-state perspective, a lack of cooperation concerning transboundary waters will have dramatic impacts on the individual, not only through a lack of water, but through various social, economic and environmental impacts. As such, various rules and principles within the law of international watercourses help to ensure access to water by these groups and minimize these negative impacts. This primarily falls onto the substantive principles of equitable and reasonable use and the due diligence obligation not to cause significant harm, however, given that they support these substantive rules, countermeasures concerning the procedural rules may also face limitations.

Given the importance of water for life and in line with the corollary duties of the duty to cooperate, certain provisions in the law of international watercourses possess a "humanitarian" character, and would arguably fall within the aforementioned restrictions to non-performance, suspension/termination and countermeasures. Non-performance of specific, correlating duties could be legal so long as it does not impact provisions of a humanitarian nature, as found in VCLT 60(5). Thus, it would likely be legal for states to respond in kind if their riparian neighbours were to violate select procedural provisions; however, it would almost certainly be considered illegal to respond in kind to violations of equitable and reasonable use or the due diligence obligation not to cause significant harm as such duties arguably protect the human individual. Similarly, the suspension or termination of a treaty in whole or in part is also likely to be legal, so long as those states continue to abide by the customary rules of equitable and reasonable use and the due diligence obligation not to cause significant harm. Whereas these restrictions primarily relate to the substantive rules, the non-performance or suspension of provisions regarding the procedural rules including prior notification, consultation and information sharing may also face restrictions. While their immediate suspension may not impact the human individual, such obligations are fundamental in upholding the substantive rules. If a state were to stop sharing information, for example, then it may be legal to reciprocally withhold hydrological information. Given the importance of information sharing to upholding the substantive rules, however, a protracted reciprocal non-performance or suspension of these provisions will make it difficult for states to maintain their compliance with equitable and reasonable use as well as the due diligence obligation not to cause significant harm.

The use of countermeasures, peaceful actions that are themselves unlawful but adopted towards the non-complying state to induce compliance, will also face limits in relation to their content and application. Although extremely unlikely to be utilized as a countermeasure, limiting water access to a neighbouring state in order to induce compliance will face limits as it will most certainly impact the human rights of citizens in neighbouring riparian states, and is extremely unlikely to meet the test of proportionality. States could do so intentionally,[2] but such restrictions of water supply are more likely to come about as an unintentional side effect of development that does not fit within the cooperative framework of the law of international watercourses. In line with this, Slovakia's implementation of Variant C was found to be unlawful as it violated Hungary's right to an equitable and reasonable share of the shared water resource. Furthermore, given the interconnectivity of shared water systems, such water-based measures are likely to have collateral impacts, particularly in upstream/downstream situations, that would infringe upon the requirement that such measures be directed at the violating state

(ARSIWA 2001: art. 49(1–2)). These water-based measures would be unlawful, but this does not leave states unable to resort to countermeasures. Given that countermeasures need not relate to the violated corresponding duty, states may be able to implement countermeasures by suspending their treaty obligations in related sectors, such as energy, trade, etc. in order to bring a violating state back into compliance. While the implementation of countermeasures in related areas may avoid collateral impacts, doing so legally may prove extremely difficult as it is easier to prove the necessity and proportionality of countermeasures which more closely resemble the original breach. This was first established in the *Air Services Agreement Arbitration,* which concerned the use of countermeasures in the same area, air services. The award stated that "all counter-measures must, in the first instance, have some degree of equivalence with the alleged breach," thus the further away in content from the original violation the more difficult it will be to establish the proportionality and necessity of the countermeasure (ICJ 1978: para. 83). This sentiment was echoed in commentary on the Draft Articles on State Responsibility (ARSIWA 2001). If, for example, a state were to seize the assets of the violating state that are under its jurisdiction in response to a breach concerning its water agreements, then it may be difficult to prove that such countermeasures are both proportionate to the violation and necessary to bring the violating state back into compliance. Suspending provisions or agreements regarding, for example, hydropower production, however, may more easily pass these tests.

Although states may, under the above-mentioned restrictions, legally resort to countermeasures, they may prove unhelpful in many instances. As Crawford states, "[b]ilateral countermeasures strongly favour states that are more powerful," and so "if weaker states are forced to resort to bilateral countermeasures without the support of interested third party states, serious breaches may go unremedied" (Crawford 2013: 704). In transboundary basins this could imply that weaker states would find themselves having to accept an allocation or harm that is unjust, and if the violating state does not consent to reciprocal dispute settlement mechanisms then it may be without remedy. In order to rectify this situation, an *earlier version* of the Draft Articles on State Responsibility permitted "any state other than the injured state" to invoke responsibility if the violated obligation is: a) "owed to a group of States including that State, and is established for the protection of a collective interest," or b) if "the obligation breached is owed to the international community as a whole" (ILC 2000: art. 49(1)). In line with this, Article 54(1) permitted that these third-party states "may take countermeasures at the request and on behalf of any State injured by the breach" (ILC 2000: art. 54(1)). As states, at the time, agreed that such measures "had only a doubtful basis in international law and would be destabilizing" (Crawford et al. 2001: 981), neither of these articles made it to the final draft in that form.[3] In spite of the fact that they are not present in the Draft Articles, they illustrate a potential path forward for states who, on their own, would be unable to enact effective countermeasures and would, therefore, be required to live with such unfairness. If the law of state responsibility were to develop in favour of collective measures as in the above-mentioned provisions, then there are two pathways in which third-party countermeasures could be implemented. First, if the duty to cooperate were to be firmly established as an obligation *erga omnes*, then, under Article 49(1b), it may be the case that third-party states could invoke the responsibility of the violating state and enact countermeasures. As an *erga omnes* obligation, the duty to cooperate would be owed to the international community as a whole, permitting others to take countermeasures at the request of the weaker state, thus providing a remedy to the situation. Second, even if the *erga omnes* status of the duty to cooperate is not accepted then it may still be possible for select third-party states to invoke state responsibility. As shared water resources are part of a collective interest and are often governed under multilateral legal frameworks, then, according to Article 49(1a), states within that framework may also be able to invoke state responsibility. Without further legal development in both the law of state responsibility and the law of international watercourses, however, such measures are unlikely to be utilized. Furthermore, it is unclear if it is advisable for states to pursue such measures, as bringing third-states into a conflict runs the risk of expanding the conflict, not resolving it.

Conclusion

The law of international watercourses is a law of cooperation, providing a framework for the joint management and allocation of shared freshwater resources. Within the law of international watercourses, such cooperation is illustrated through the general duty to cooperate as well as the substantive and procedural rules which govern transboundary waters. Such rules follow a reciprocal structure of equal rights and duties for all parties, ensuring a process of cooperation which is fair and balanced. Aiming to find peaceful solutions through consultation, the procedural rules act as a method of dispute avoidance. They are, however, not always successful and when disputes arise states can, given mutual consent, pursue a series of diplomatic and judicial means to settle their dispute.

The same can be said of the procedural rules found in bilateral treaties to which China is party, which strictly adhere to a reciprocal structure of rights and duties, except in certain instances of unilateral information sharing between China and some of its southern neighbours. Such actions work to build trust in the hope of future cooperation and ultimately institutionalization through legal mechanisms. As noted above, China does not adhere to third-party mechanisms of dispute settlement, preferring to pursue friendly consultation and negotiation based on reciprocity. This may create issues for states given that China is an upstream superpower, but as China increasingly depends on its neighbours for its own prosperity, its riparians are in a strong position to use issue-linkage in order to level the playing field. This reciprocal framework is apparent in developing cooperation on the Lancang-Mekong River through the LMC Mechanism. Although aspects of the discussion surrounding this mechanism reflect various procedural rules, there is a lack of clarity as to how such cooperation will be conducted and the potential overlap between the LMC and other regional institutions. A focus on reciprocity via the reciprocal rights and duties and balanced advantages and disadvantages of the parties will assist in its development. For example, as cooperation unfolds it would be highly beneficial for states to formalize information sharing through some kind of agreement which outlines the rights and duties of the parties. Fully implementing a reciprocal approach with balanced rights and duties for all would go a long way to building trust, furthering the positive momentum witnessed in the region. However, even though the emergence of a reciprocal structure can be seen in the LMC Mechanism, China's long-term intentions remain unclear and it has yet to be seen how cooperation based on the principles it embodies will work in practice.

Within general international law states have the ability and legal right to resort to a variety of reciprocity-based self-help measures when there has been a violation of the norms of international law. The importance of transboundary water resources provides the impetus for cooperation and compliance; this, however, may also point to the necessity to ensure compliance via self-help measures. There is, however, limited practice surrounding such measures within the law of international watercourses and even a tendency to shy away from such adversarial and confrontational mechanisms. Instead, courts often refer the parties to continued negotiations in good faith, as was seen in the *Gabčíkovo-Nagymaros Case* and *San Juan Case*. Whereas other authors have pointed to the indeterminacy of the substantive rules or the normative nature of the procedural rules to explain this, this chapter looked to the duty to cooperate and the possibility that it is an emerging obligation *erga omnes* to provide insight into the limitations such measures face. Such obligations are no longer bilateralizable as they are not owed to individual states, but to the international community. As a potential emerging *erga omnes* obligation that is intrinsically connected to the human aspects of water, it signals the humanization of the law of international watercourses. While states could enact non-performance and suspension/termination, it has been illustrated that such measures cannot violate the substantive rules of equitable and reasonable use, and the due diligence obligation not to cause significant harm as they arguably have a humanitarian character. Furthermore, even though states may suspend their performance of various procedural rules, their protracted non-performance or suspension is likely to face these humanitarian limitations, as they are fundamental in upholding the substantive rules of the law of international watercourses.

Water-based countermeasures are almost certainly illegal, but given the interconnectivity of transboundary water resources countermeasures in other areas may be pursued. Their legality, however, may be difficult to prove as they must pass the tests of proportionality and necessity. Although they may be legal, countermeasures have been characterized as favouring the powerful over the weak, and without the support of third parties, weaker states are unlikely to find remedy through such reciprocal measures. Given that the duty to cooperate is a potential emerging obligation *erga omnes* it may be possible for third-party states to invoke state responsibility on their behalf; however, this would require significant developments in both the law of international watercourses and the law of state responsibility.

Acknowledgements

A version of this chapter first appeared as an article in *Natural Resources Journal*. For the original article, see Devlaeminck, David J. (2019). The Legal Principle of Reciprocity in the Peaceful Management of Transboundary Watercourses: Exploring the Duty to Cooperate, Rules of Procedure and Self-Help Measures. *Natural Resources Journal*, 59(2), 301-320. Sections of this chapter also appeared in the *Chinese Journal of Environmental Law*. For the original article, see Devlaeminck, D. J. (2018). The Legal Principle of Reciprocity and China's Water Treaty Practice. *Chinese Journal of Environmental Law*, 2(2), 195–222.

Notes

1 It should be noted that the UNECE adopted the Protocol on Civil Liability and Compensation for Damage Caused by the Transboundary Effects of Industrial Accidents on Transboundary Waters to the UNECE Water Convention in 2003; however, it is not yet in force as only one state (Hungary) has adopted it. It permits individuals harmed by transboundary impact to make claims for compensation, however, states it "shall not affect the rights and obligations of the Parties under the rules of general international law with respect to the international responsibility of States" (UNECE 2003).

2 Instances of such actions are extremely rare and unlikely to ever be used as a countermeasure designed to induce compliance and ensure future cooperative relations. For example, in 1947 India cut off water to Pakistan via select canals at the height of a dispute, ultimately resulting in the establishment of the Dominion Accords. If carried out today, even if utilized as a countermeasure, they almost certainly would not meet the test of proportionality and necessity, nor would they abide by the restrictions on countermeasures found in ARSIWA, Article 50(1).

3 The final version includes Article 48 – *Invocation of responsibility by a State other than the injured State*, which permits states other than the injured state to invoke the responsibility of breaches for obligations that are owed to a group that includes that state, or of obligations owed to the international community as a whole. Article 54 then goes on to indicate that these states may take "lawful measures against that State to ensure cessation of the breach and reparation in the interest of the injured State." The use of the word "lawful" does not preclude the use of countermeasures, but leaves this issue open for further development.

References

ARSIWA (2001). Draft Articles on Responsibility of States for Internationally Wrongful Acts with Commentaries. Retrieved from https://legal.un.org/ilc/texts/instruments/english/commentaries/9_6_2001.pdf

Axelrod, R. & Keohane, R. O. (1985). Achieving Cooperation Under Anarchy: Strategies and Institutions. *World Politics*, *28*(1), 226–54.

Bangladesh–China (2010). Joint Statement between the People's Republic of China and the People's Republic of Bangladesh (adopted March 21, 2010).

Byers, M. (1997). Conceptualising the Relationship between Jus Cogens and Erga Omnes Rules. *Nordic Journal of International Law*, *66*, 211–39.

Canelas de Castro, P. (2015). The Evolution of International Water Law. *International Journal of Sustainable Development Planning*, *10*(6), 894–900.

China–India (2014). Implementation Plan Between India and China for Yarlung Tsangpo and Brahmaputra River (adopted September 19, 2014).

China–India (2018). Memorandum of Understanding between Ministry of Water Resources, The People's Republic of China and Ministry of Water Resources, River Development and Ganga Rejuvenation, Republic of India upon provision of hydrological information of the Brahmaputra river in flood season by China to India (signed June 9, 2018).

China–Kazakhstan (2001). Agreement on Cooperation in the Use and Protection of Transboundary Rivers (signed February 22, 2001).

China–Mongolia (1994). Agreement on the Protection and Utilization of Transboundary Waters (signed April 29, 1993).

Crawford, J. (2013). *State Responsibility: The General Part*. Cambridge: Cambridge University Press.

Crawford, J., Peel, J. & Olleson, S. (2001). The ILC's Articles on Responsibility of States for International Wrongful Acts: Completion of the Second Reading. *European Journal of International Law*, *12*(5), 963–91.

Daoudy, M. (2009). Asymmetric Power: Negotiating Water in the Euphrates and Tigris. *International Negotiation*, *14*, 361–91.

Fard, S. N. (2016). *Reciprocity in International Law: Its Impact and Function*. Abingdon/New York: Routledge.

Ho, S. (2017). China's Transboundary River Policies Towards Kazakhstan: Issue-Linkages and Incentives for Cooperation *Water International*, *42*(2), 142–62.

ICJ (1945). Statute of the International Court of Justice (adopted October 24, 1945).

ICJ (1970). Case Concerning the Barcelona Traction, Light and Power Company (Belgium v. Spain) (International Court of Justice, February 5, 1970).

ICJ (1978). Case concerning the Air Service Agreement of March 27, 1946 (United States of America v. France) (Arbitral Tribunal, December 9, 1978).

ICJ (1997a). Case Concerning the Gabčíkovo-Nagymaros Project (Hungary v. Slovakia) – Judgement (International Court of Justice, September 25, 1997).

ICJ (1997b). Case Concerning the Gabčíkovo-Nagymaros Project (Hungary v. Slovakia) – Dissenting Opinion of Judge Vereshchetin (International Court of Justice, September 25, 1997).

ICJ (2010). Case Concerning Pulp Mills on the River Uruguay – (Argentina v. Uruguay) – Judgement (International Court of Justice, April 20, 2010).

ICJ (2011). Application of the Interim Accord of September 13, 1995 (The Former Yugoslav Republic of Macedonia v. Greece) – Separate Opinion of Judge Bruno Simma (International Court of Justice, December 5, 2011).

ICJ (2015). Certain Activities Carried out by Nicaragua in the Border Area (Costa Rica v. Nicaragua)/Construction of a Road in Costa Rica Along the San Juan River

(Nicaragua v. Costa Rica) – Judgement (International Court of Justice, December 16, 2015).

ICTY (2000). Prosecutor v. Kupreškić et al. (International Criminal Tribunal for the Prosecution of Persons Responsible for Serious Violations of International Humanitarian Law Committed in the Territory of the Former Yugoslavia, January 14, 2000).

ILC (1994). *The Law of Non-Navigational Uses of International Watercourses: Draft articles and commentaries thereto adopted by the Drafting Committee on second reading*, A/CN.4/L.493 (July 8, 1994). Retrieved from https://documents-dds-ny.un.org/doc/UNDOC/LTD/G94/630/22/pdf/G9463022.pdf?OpenElement

ILC (2000). *State Responsibility – Draft Articles Provisionally Adopted by the Drafting Committee on Second Reading*, A/CN.4/L.600 (August 21, 2000). Retrieved from https://documents-dds-ny.un.org/doc/UNDOC/LTD/G00/632/25/pdf/G0063225.pdf?OpenElement

Lammers, J. G. (1998). The Gabčíkovo-Nagymaros Case Seen in Particular From the Perspective of the Law of International Watercourses and the Protection of the Environment. *Leiden Journal of International Law, 11*, 287–320.

Lammers, J. G. (2014). The Helsinki Water Convention: A New Implementation Mechanism and Committee. *Environmental Policy and Law, 44*(1–2), 117–24.

Leb, C. (2012). The Right to Water in a Transboundary Context: Emergence of Seminal Trends. *Water International, 37*(6), 640–53.

Leb, C. (2013). *Cooperation in the Law of Transboundary Water Resources*. Cambridge: Cambridge University Press.

Leb, C. (2019). Data Innovations for Transboundary Freshwater Resources Management: Are Obligations Related to Information Exchange Still Needed?. *International Water Law, 4*(4), 3–78.

Lefeber, R. (1998). The Gabčíkovo-Nagymaros Project and the Law of State Responsibility. *Leiden Journal of International Law, 6*(9), 609–23.

LMC (2016). Sanya Declaration of the First Lancang-Mekong Cooperation (LMC) Leaders' Meeting (adopted March 23, 2016).

LMC (2018a). Five-Year Plan of Action on Lancang-Mekong Cooperation (2018–2022). *China Daily* – January 11. Retrieved from www.chinadaily.com.cn/a/201801/11/WS5a56cd04a3102e5b17374295.html

LMC (2018b). Phnom Penh Declaration of the Second Lancang-Mekong Cooperation (LMC) Leaders' Meeting (adopted January 10, 2018).

LMC (2020). Vientiane Declaration of the Third Lancang-Mekong Cooperation (LMC) Leader's Meeting (adopted August 24, 2020).

LMC–MRC (2019). Memorandum of Understanding Between the Mekong River Commission Secretariat and the Lancang-Mekong Water Resources Cooperation Center (signed December 17, 2019).

McCaffrey, S. (2019). *The Law of International Watercourses* (3 ed.). Oxford: Oxford University Press.

McIntyre, O. (2011). The World Court's Ongoing Contribution to International Water Law: The Pulp Mills Case between Argentina and Uruguay. *Water Alternatives, 3*(2), 123–44.

McIntyre, O. (2017). Water, Law and Equity. In D. Devlaeminck, Z. Adeel & R. Sandford (Eds.), *The Human Face of Water Security*. Cham: Springer.

McIntyre, O. (2019). Responsibility and Liability in International Law for Damage to Transboundary Fresh Water Resources. In M. Tignino, G. Pflieger & C. Brethaut (Eds.), *Research Handbook on Freshwater Law and International Relations* (pp. 338–68). Cheltenham: Edward Elgar.

MWR (2014). India-China Cooperation. *Ministry of Water Resources of India.* Retrieved from http://wrmin.nic.in/forms/list.aspx?lid=349

MRC (2008). Agreement on provision of hydrological information renewed by China and MRC. *Mekong River Commission.* Retrieved from www.mrcmekong.org/news-and-events/news/agreement-on-provision-of-hydrological-information-renewed-by-china-and-mrc/

MRC (2018a). China Notified About Discharge of Jinghong Reservoir 5 Days in Advance. *Mekong River Commission* – April 4. Retrieved from www.mrcmekong.org/news-and-events/news/press-release-mrc-escir-3/

MRC (2018b). Water Flow in Jinghong to Decrease, but Without Significant Impact Downstream. *Mekong River Commission* – August 14. Retrieved from www.mrcmekong.org/news-and-events/news/water-flow-in-jinghong-to-decrease-but-without-significant-impact-downstream/

MRC (2019a). Mekong Water Levels to Drop Due to Dam Equipment Testing in China. *Mekong River Commission* – December 31. Retrieved from www.mrcmekong.org/news-and-events/news/mekong-water-levels-to-drop-due-to-dam-equipment-testing-in-china/

MRC (2019b). MRC and China Renew Pact on Water Data Provision and Other Cooperative Initiatives. *Mekong River Commission* – July 19. Retrieved from www.mrcmekong.org/news-and-events/news/mrc-and-china-renew-pact-on-water-data-provision-and-other-cooperation-initiatives/

MRC (2019c). Water Flow in Jinghong of China to Decrease, but Without Significant Impact Downstream. *Mekong River Commission* – April 8. Retrieved from www.mrcmekong.org/news-and-events/news/water-flow-in-jinghong-of-china-to-decrease-but-without-significant-impact-downstream/

Osiel, M. (2009). *The End of Reciprocity: Terror, Torture and the Law of War.* Cambridge: Cambridge University Press.

Pauwelyn, J. (2003). A Typology of Multilateral Treaty Obligations: Are WTO Obligations Bilateral or Collective in Nature? *European Journal of International Law, 14*(5), 907–51.

Ragazzi, M. (2002). *The Concept of International Obligations Erga Omnes.* Oxford: Oxford University Press.

Su, Y. (2014). Contemporary Legal Analysis of China's Transboundary Water Regimes: International Law in Practice. *Water International, 39*(5), 705–24.

Tanzi, A. & Contartese, C. (2015). Dispute Prevention, Dispute Settlement and Implementation Facilitation in International Water Law: The Added Value of the Establishment of an Implementation Mechanisms under the Water Convention. In A. Tanzi, O. McIntyre, A. Kolliopoulos, A. Rieu-Clarke & R. Kinna (Eds.), *The UNECE Convention on the Protection and Use of Transboundary Watercourses and International Lakes: Its Contribution to International Water Cooperation* (pp. 319–29). Leiden: Brill-Nijhoff.

Tanzi, A. & Milano, E. (2013). Article 33 of the UN Watercourses Convention: A Step Forward for Dispute Settlement? *Water International, 38*(2), 166–79.

UN Charter (1945). Charter of the United Nations (adopted June 26, 1945; entered into force October 24, 1945).

UNECE (2003). Protocol on Civil Liability and Compensation for Damage Caused by the Transboundary Effects of Industrial Accidents on Transboundary Waters to the UNECE Water Convention (signed May 21, 2003).

UNECE (2012a). *Decision and Vision for the Future of the Convention – Decision VI/I Support to Implementation and Compliance*, ECE/MP.WAT/37/Add.2 (September 19, 2013). Retrieved from https://documents-dds-ny.un.org/doc/UNDOC/GEN/G13/249/52/pdf/G1324952.pdf?OpenElement

UNECE (2012b). *Draft Decision on Support to Implementation and Compliance*, ECE/MP.WAT/2012/L.4 (September 14, 2012). Retrieved from https://documents-dds-ny.un.org/doc/UNDOC/LTD/G12/243/14/pdf/G1224314.pdf?OpenElement

UNECE (2013). *Guide to Implementing the Water Convention*, ECE/MP.WAT/39 (September 2013). Retrieved from www.unece.org/fileadmin/DAM/env/water/publications/WAT_Guide_to_implementing_Convention/ECE_MP.WAT_39_Guide_to_implementing_water_convention_small_size_ENG.pdf

UNGA (1997). *99th Plenary Meeting, United Nations General Assembly*, A/51/PV.99 (May 21, 1997). Retrieved from https://documents-dds-ny.un.org/doc/UNDOC/GEN/N97/855/72/pdf/N9785572.pdf?OpenElement

UNSC (2016). *Maintenance of International Peace and Security: Water, Peace and Security* S/PV.7818 (November 22, 2016). Retrieved from https://documents-dds-ny.un.org/doc/UNDOC/PRO/N16/396/80/pdf/N1639680.pdf?OpenElement

VCLT (1969). Vienna Convention on the Law of Treaties (adopted May 23, 1969; entered into force January 27, 1980).

Villiger, M. E. (2009). *Commentary on the 1969 Vienna Convention on the Law of Treaties*. Leiden: Martinus Nijhoff.

Water Convention (1992). Convention on the Protection and Use of Transboundary Watercourses and International Lakes (adopted on March 17, 1992; entered into force October 6, 1996).

Watercourses Convention (1997). United Nations Convention on the Law of Non-Navigational Uses of International Watercourses (adopted on May 21, 1997; entered into force August 17, 2014).

Williams, J. M. (2020). Is Three a Crowd? River Basin Institutions and the Governance of the Mekong River. *International Journal of Water Resources Development*. doi:10.1080/07900627.2019.1700779

Wouters, P. (2013). *International Law – Facilitating Transboundary Water Cooperation*. GWP TEC. Retrieved from www.gwp.org/globalassets/global/toolbox/publications/background-papers/17-international-law--facilitating-transboundary-water-cooperation-2013-english.pdf

Wouters, P. (2014). The Yin and Yang of International Water Law: China's Transboundary Water Practice and the Changing Contours of Sovereignty. *RECIEL*, *23*(1), 67–75.

Wouters, P. & Chen, H. (2013). China's "Soft-Path" to Transboundary Water Cooperation Examined in the Light of Two UN Global Water Conventions–Exploring the "Chinese Way." *Journal of Water Law*, *22*(6), 229–47.

Wouters, P. & Leb, C. (2015). The Duty to Cooperate in International Law – Examining the Contribution of the UN Water Conventions to Facilitating Transboundary

Water Cooperation. In A. Tanzi, O. McIntyre, A. Kolliopoulos, A. Rieu-Clarke & R. Kinna (Eds.), *The UNECE Convention on the Protection and Use of Transboundary Watercourses and International Lakes* (pp. 285–95). Leiden: Brill-Nijhoff.

Wouters, P. & Tarlock, A. D. (2013). The Third Wave of Normativity in Global Water Law: The Duty to Cooperate in the Peaceful Management of the World's Water Resources: An Emerging Obligation Erga Omnes? *Journal of Water Law, 23*, 51–65.

Zartman, I. W. & Touval, S. (2011). Introduction: Return to the Theories of Cooperation. In I. W. Zartman & S. Touval (Eds.), *International Cooperation: The Extents and Limits of Multilateralism* (pp. 1–14). Cambridge: Cambridge University Press.

6 Observations and concluding remarks

Reciprocity, a roughly equivalent and contingent exchange, permeates international law and transboundary water relations. Whether states are upstream, midstream or downstream, their actions, in one way or another, impact their riparian neighbours. China, upstream on the majority of its transboundary waters and seeking further development at its borders, will continue to face challenges concerning the development of its transboundary waters: How can it use these waters to meet its own needs while taking into consideration the needs and interests of downstream developing states? Reciprocity, a fundamental legal principle underlying international law, provides one path to resolve this dilemma. A Chinese proverb says: "when big rivers have water, the small ones are filled; and when small rivers have water, the big ones are filled." Quoted by Xi Jinping at the 2015 Boao Forum (Xi 2015), this brings together the message of cooperation put forward by China as its influence on the global stage continues to grow. Recognizing the interdependence and interconnectivity of states and their transboundary waters, a reciprocal approach can offer a pathway for China and its neighbours to jointly manage their transboundary waters and meet their water needs. As shown in this book, the legal principle of reciprocity has played, and continues to play, a strong role within the law of international watercourses and China's legal practice. It has shaped the law of international watercourses by placing limitations on state claims, while also ensuring a balance between the rights and duties of state parties across the key elements of transboundary water management. At a time where the rules in this field continue to evolve to meet new challenges, leading to some uncertainty surrounding the global water conventions, the bedrock principle of reciprocity offers a powerful lens to review, reassess and recalibrate the norms of the law of international watercourses.

China's relationship with international law, a system it perceives as largely designed by the West, has faced challenges and continues to evolve. As it does so, China has increasingly engaged with international law and is now present and often centre-stage at nearly every international forum, seeking to engage with international law development and becoming party to a number of multilateral treaties. This did not occur overnight, but is the result of a slow and incremental approach supported by China's emphasis on the Five

Principles and its support for the UN Charter, specifically its unwavering respect for state sovereignty and mutual benefit. China, like other upstream states, had serious concerns about the law of international watercourses and its ability to protect its interests. Utilizing the legal principle of reciprocity, this book, however, has illustrated that the law of international watercourses, with its roots in the notion of limited territorial sovereignty, codified and progressively developed in both the 1997 United Nations Convention on the Law of the Non-navigational Uses of International Watercourses (Watercourses Convention) and the 1992 United Nations Economic Commission for Europe (UNECE) Convention on the Protection and Use of Transboundary Watercourses and International Lakes (Water Convention), in many ways offers a fair and balanced reciprocal framework of corresponding rights and duties.

Most importantly, the reciprocal approach exemplified in the law of international watercourses is capable of protecting the interests of both upstream and downstream states as it ensures corresponding rights and duties between riparians. This is apparent across the entire range of rules established by the global water conventions, firmly founded on limited territorial sovereignty and reciprocal rule structures found in the substantive rules, duty to cooperate, procedural rules and dispute settlement mechanisms. Together, they provide a mutually supportive and reciprocal process through which states can jointly determine an equitable and reasonable use of waters while meeting the due diligence obligation not to cause significant transboundary harm. A closer look at China's practice shows striking similarities between the reciprocal approach of the global water conventions and China's own practice. As an upstream riparian, China could, hypothetically speaking, act unilaterally and claim absolute territorial sovereignty. The reciprocal process through which international water law has developed and both the positive and negative aspects of reciprocity, however, make it unlikely to do so. In other words, reciprocity ensures that states are more likely to limit their own actions in consideration of their neighbours, rather than selfishly develop their transboundary waters, due in part to considerations of their own long-term interests and the potential for repercussions. In this vein, China has sought to limit its own development and contour its transboundary water relations via various bilateral agreements and related documents with its neighbours through which it takes the interests of all parties into consideration, including its own domestic needs and concerns. Although they vary in scope, many of China's bilateral transboundary water agreements broadly align with the overarching norms of the law of international watercourses and are consistent with China's approach to international law based on the Five Principles.

The inclusion of these norms in China's practice often, but not always, involves a strong emphasis on reciprocity, aiming to ensure that its rights and obligations are fair and balanced. This can be said of the substantive and procedural rules in agreements to which China is party. Some agreements and select provisions, however, while on their face appearing to be non-reciprocal in nature, i.e. where China agrees to share hydrological information with downstream riparians, in fact, are founded on the very notion of reciprocity. In line with its commitment to the Five Principles, as China expands its engagement with its neighbours, these types of agreements deepen practical engagement and work to enhance trust. This is an important building block towards greater cooperation and potentially even the forebearer for the future establishment of more comprehensive transboundary water agreements. China continues to follow the Five Principles, emphasizing reciprocity through the mutual respect for sovereignty, non-aggression, non-interference and mutual benefit in the pursuit of peaceful coexistence. These elements are revealed in China's bilateral approach to transboundary water management and the way they impact reciprocity. Although China's transboundary water agreements reflect reciprocity in many ways, in furthering the peaceful management of transboundary waters, an increased emphasis on more pragmatic reciprocity could help to fully implement the Five Principles. In the context of China, key to this is a reciprocal understanding of the substantive rules, particularly that harm flows both downstream and upstream.

In striving to manage shared water resources, states must come together to jointly determine an equitable and reasonable allocation of uses, capable of ongoing re-evaluation and adjustment. Transboundary watercourse states have both the *right* to an equitable and reasonable utilization of the freshwater resources in their territory and the *duty* to exercise due diligence in their efforts not to cause significant harm in their management of these shared waters. In line with its approach to international law, China's transboundary water agreements often take a limited territorial sovereignty approach. Despite this, gaps remain and provision to take into consideration the downstream impact of its upstream development activities are not fully fleshed out in the agreements studied here. Reciprocity in China's transboundary water agreements could also better reflect the dualistic nature of harmful uses – from upstream to downstream but also downstream to upstream. This could be achieved through more complete and detailed agreements between China and its neighbours, taking on board some of the elements such as the suite of substantive rules, procedural rules, and dispute settlement mechanisms. These elements could contribute to concretizing the protection of its interests and the reciprocity that China seeks to achieve.

In recognition of upstream rights to utilization and the potential for harm to flow upstream, the procedural rules must also be implemented reciprocally. Upstream states have just as much of an interest as downstream states in receiving information from their riparian neighbours, not because it could be used to mitigate damage from heavy rains upstream, for example, but because it would allow for upstream states to have a better picture of downstream water use to best plan their own water uses and fulfil their obligations of due diligence. Although downstream developments do not necessarily have physical impacts on upstream, in recognition that downstream uses may place limitations on uses upstream, downstream states should also notify upstream states of their planned measures. China's transboundary water agreements rarely include an obligation to notify, in line with an emphasis on the mutual respect for sovereignty and mutual non-interference. If this obligation were to be implemented in recognition of this, upstream states might more readily accept it as part of their own practice, viewing it as supportive of their rights to utilize and assisting in fulfilling their due diligence obligation, not merely as an obstacle or objection to upstream development. Any consultations triggered by such notifications might be atypical, related more so to the joint achievement of a basin-wide equitable and reasonable utilization of available water resources and not necessarily related to the specific project that triggered the notification. These joint actions could be channelled through and facilitated by joint institutions which can act as hubs for reciprocal exchange, an area where China has some experience.

A reciprocal exchange need not be explicit in all agreements or provisions, most notably those that concern global community interests, such as the environment and human rights. Some of China's treaties reflect this, aiming to protect from pollution or emphasizing sustainability and other obligations similar to those agreed to in the numerous multilateral agreements that China is party to. We must, however, be conscious of a potential imbalance of obligations and benefits from protecting these community interests, requiring states to explore innovative ways to share the benefits of joint water management and rebalance them in relation to state obligations. With the impact of climate change and the fact that many of Asia's major rivers are fed by glaciers in the Tibetan Plateau, this will have significant relevance for China. China, however, has become party to a variety of multilateral environmental and human rights agreements in the past, which may provide examples of best practice in implementing these kinds of obligations.

Although many of China's transboundary waters are shared by China and more than one state, bilateralism has been a successful and useful strategy for China thus far. It has even been suggested that, given China's preference for bilateralism, it may be more appropriate for China and its neighbours to adopt bilateral agreements even when it concerns transboundary water resources with more than two riparians (Ibrahim 2019). Although China's bilateralist approach has seen some success, these multilateral river basins have posed significant challenges for China. In this regard, it may be beneficial to move towards a multilateral approach that is capable of managing the "basin," the "practical hydrological unit for water resources management" (GWP & INBO 2009). In terms of their legal rights and obligations, however, multilateral agreements and bilateral agreements are not so different, and both can be characterized as reciprocal, bilateral legal relations or bundles thereof. China has already made a series of moves towards multilateralism in relation to other areas of international law, particularly economic and environmental law, and it appears to be experimenting with multilateralism on its transboundary waters.

The Lancang-Mekong River, where China has established the Lancang-Mekong Cooperation (LMC) Mechanism, is one such example. On the Lancang-Mekong there is increasing evidence that upstream hydropower dams are having an impact on downstream states and the health of the basin as a whole. The exact extent and contours of this impact, however, continues to be the topic of discussion, but as the impact of climate change increases across the region these impacts may become more acute. In regards to this debate, there have been calls for "a more institutionalized arrangement" that will be capable of addressing "risks that can only be managed through a 'whole-of-basin' approach" (MRC 2020). Given China's reluctance to join the Mekong River Commission, could this be the LMC? Throughout this book, it has been illustrated that the LMC Mechanism and related documents include hints of both the substantive and procedural norms of the law of international watercourses. The relatively new LMC does not specifically mention rules or principles regarding the allocation of water resources or the prevention of harm; however, the participating states aim generally to "enhance cooperation [...] in sustainable water resources management and utilization" (LMC 2016: para. 10). Whether it has agreed to these rules or not, the LMC and related projects are in some ways bound by international water law norms given their status as customary international law, and due to its member states engagement with these norms via the 1995 Agreement on the Cooperation for the Sustainable Development of the Mekong. In order to establish itself as a multilateral water governance mechanism, however, the LMC requires significant normative, procedural and institutional development, a process that could greatly benefit from an emphasis on reciprocity.

The global water conventions could provide one such avenue for the normative development of the joint management of China's transboundary waters. As this book has illustrated, China's legal practice is largely in line with the reciprocal process found in the global water conventions, and the norms of the law of international watercourses are capable of protecting China's upstream interests. If this is the case, then we must ask ourselves why China has not moved to accede to either one or both of the global water conventions. They are both open for accession if China wishes to do so, and accession could provide significant benefits for China.

Acceding to the global water conventions could insert much-needed legal clarity into China's transboundary water agreements. China's agreements follow a similar structure as the global water conventions; however, it is often the case, as illustrated throughout this study, that the language used in China's transboundary water treaties is vague in comparison, potentially leading to problems of interpretation and implementation. Given their status as framework conventions, accession to them would be a clear recognition of the norms within, ensuring that China's current agreements could be interpreted in light of the global water conventions. In this regard, the Watercourses Convention is probably more appealing as, unlike the Water Convention, which requires states to harmonize their agreements, it would not obligate China to harmonize existing agreements with the Convention (Water Convention 1992: art 3(1); Watercourses Convention 1997: art. 9(1)). Any future agreements that China would establish, however, would need to align with the provisions of that instrument.

Accession could provide a stable legal regime through which to govern China's transboundary waters, building trust between China and its neighbours. Acceding to the global water conventions and, if necessary, harmonizing existing or future agreements, would ensure that all of China's vast transboundary waters, shared with its 17 riparian neighbours, fall under the same or similar legal regime (in cases of pre-existing agreements), in which all states have the same or similar reciprocal rights and obligations. With significant issues of trust between China and its neighbours, particularly in the Southwest, a common legal framework that reflects the current status of the law of international watercourses could provide the common platform needed to ensure stable and long-lasting relationships upon which to build trust.

Accession could also provide a framework for state relations beyond its borders, assisting in China's "going out" process, Belt and Road Initiative and good neighbour policy. As China has emerged on the global stage as a rising power, it has taken on an increasingly prominent role in the international community through various Chinese-led initiatives. But as its prominence in the world increases, so too will the necessity of engagement with states who, in one form or another, are bound by the global water conventions. Of the 76 members of the Asian Infrastructure Investment Bank, for example, over a third are party to one or both of the global water conventions, jointly holding a significant voting share and influencing Bank decisions. Of the 72 states that have been identified as participants in Belt and Road projects, nearly half are party to the global water conventions (Devlaeminck & Huang 2020). It is likely that as these initiatives grow and more states join, that the influence of the global water conventions on them would grow as well. Not only is China finding itself working with states that are bound by, and abide by, these norms, but China, Chinese companies and Chinese nationals are working on and investing in projects around the world in states that are bound by these norms. This is apparent in China's involvement in global hydropower development, for example, involved in approximately 38% of all completed, under construction or at the MoU level, hydropower projects in Southeast Asia (Williams 2019). China's investment, lending and infrastructure initiatives are bound to have an impact on the utilization of transboundary watercourses at one point or another, and accession to either of the global water conventions could provide a common understanding of how best to engage in these projects and overseas relations.

Although there might be significant benefits that China would receive by acceding to the global water conventions, significant obstacles remain, such as the compulsory dispute settlement mechanisms set forth in those global instruments. Consistent with its approach to international law, China does not accept compulsory dispute settlement, preferring consultation or negotiation for the settlement of disputes on a case-by-case basis. Given its recent experience in the South China Sea arbitration, its attitude towards third-party dispute settlement is unlikely to change (Zhang & Li 2018). With this in mind, the Watercourses Convention and mandatory fact-finding (1997: art. 33(3–9)) would not be palatable to China, while the formula under the Water Convention, which does not include any mandatory dispute settlement mechanisms (1992: art. 22), might be more agreeable. Regardless of specific provisions, China could submit a reservation, effectively establishing a reciprocal limitation on that obligation, as Vietnam has done in regards to dispute settlement under the Watercourses Convention. Such reservations are permitted under the Vienna Convention on the Law of Treaties, provided they are not explicitly prohibited by the treaty and are compatible with the treaty's object and purpose (1969: art. 19). Without adequate mechanisms of dispute prevention and settlement, China and its neighbours have limited options to ensure compliance with their treaty provisions. Despite this, there are a range of diplomatic and institutional mechanisms that could help with promoting ongoing peaceful transboundary relations.

A single overarching transboundary water cooperation framework between China and its neighbours would be a massive step for China and also for Asia. If China were to accede to one or both of the global water conventions it would join its riparian neighbours Kazakhstan and Russia, both party to the Water Convention, and Vietnam, who is party to the Watercourses Convention. In spite of the similarities between the global water conventions, China's practice and the benefits of accession, it seems unlikely, at least in the short term, that China will accede to either global instrument. Any possible accession will require an extensive process of study and consideration on the legal and practical impacts. While this book has provided some insights into China's possible next steps in the area of transboundary water cooperation through the legal notion of reciprocity, clearly, more research on this topic would be welcome. A renewed focus on legal reciprocity could help to reinvigorate nation-state engagement with international law around the world. Over a period of a few decades, China has gone from a state largely unfamiliar and cautious regarding the international legal system, to one of the most important international legal actors of today. As China's relationship with international law continues to evolve, its engagement has been, and will be continue to be, fuelled by an emphasis on reciprocity via the Five Principles, and support for the United Nations and its Charter. As China seeks continued development and pursues its good neighbour policy, reciprocity will continue to be an important mainstay of its approach to broader inter-state relations. Further opportunities for improved transboundary water cooperation and the achievement of peaceful coexistence between China and its riparian neighbours will emerge from the joint management of its transboundary waters and its engagement with international law.

References

Devlaeminck, D. J. & Huang, X. (2020). China and the Global Water Conventions in Light of Recent Developments: Time to take a second look?. *Review of European, Comparative and International Environmental Law 29*(3).

GWP & INBO (2009). *A Handbook for Integrated Water Resources Management in Basins.* Global Water Partnership and International Network of River Basin Organizations. Retrieved from www.inbo-news.org/IMG/pdf/GWP-INBOHandbookForIWRMinBasins.pdf

Ibrahim, I. A. (2019). Water Governance in the Mekong After the Watercourses Convention 35th Ratification: Multilateral or Bilateral Approach?. *International Journal of Water Resources Development, 36*(1), 200–20.

MRC (2020). *Understanding the Mekong River's Hydrological Conditions: A brief commentary note on the "Monitoring the Quantity of Water Flowing Through the Upper Mekong Basin Under Natural (Unimpeded) Conditions" study by Alan Basist and Claude Williams.* Mekong River Commission. Retrieved from www.mrcmekong.org/assets/Publications/Understanding-Mekong-River-hydrological-conditions_2020.pdf

LMC (2016). Sanya Declaration of the First Lancang-Mekong Cooperation (LMC) Leaders' Meeting (adopted March 23, 2016).

VCLT (1969). Vienna Convention on the Law of Treaties (adopted May 23, 1969; entered into force January 27, 1980).

Water Convention (1992). Convention on the Protection and Use of Transboundary Watercourses and International Lakes (adopted on March 17, 1992; entered into force October 6, 1996).

Watercourses Convention (1997). United Nations Convention on the Law of Non-Navigational Uses of International Watercourses (adopted on May 21, 1997; entered into force August 17, 2014).

Williams, J. M. (2019). Emerging Costs of China's Belt and Road Strategy for Transboundary Water in South and Southeast Asia. *International Journal of Water Resources Development, 3*, 81–92.

Xi, J. (2015). Towards a Community of Common Destiny and a New Future for Asia, Keynote Speech, Boao Forum for Asia Annual Conference – March 28. Retrieved from http://news.xinhuanet.com/english/2015-03/29/c_134106145.htm

Zhang, H. & Li, M. (2018). China and Global Water Governance: New Developments. In H. Zhang & M. Li (Eds.), *China and Transboundary Water Politics in Asia* (pp. 219–37). Abingdon/New York: Routledge.

Index

For Product Safety Concerns and Information please contact our EU representative GPSR@taylorandfrancis.com
Taylor & Francis Verlag GmbH, Kaufingerstraße 24, 80331 München, Germany

www.ingramcontent.com/pod-product-compliance
Lightning Source LLC
LaVergne TN
LVHW021131300926
849160LV00010B/963

* 9 7 8 0 3 6 7 6 1 5 9 7 0 *